www.ChildCareE...

Exchange
The Early Childhood Leaders' Magazine Since 1978

Play

A Beginnings Workshop Book

Edited by Bonnie Neugebauer

PLAY

A Beginnings Workshop Book

These articles were collected from the Beginnings Workshop feature of *Exchange —
The Early Childhood Leaders' Magazine*. Every attempt has been made to update information
on authors and other contributors to these articles. We apologize for any biographical
information that is not current.

Exchange is a bimonthly management magazine for directors and owners of early childhood
programs. For more information about *Exchange* and other Exchange publications for
directors and teachers, contact:

Exchange
PO Box 3249
Redmond, WA 98073-3249
(800) 221-2864
www.ChildCareExchange.com

ISBN 978-0-942702-39-5

Printed in the United States of America

© Exchange Press, Inc., 2007

Cover Photograph by Bonnie Neugebauer

PLAY

A Beginnings Workshop Book

MAKE-BELIEVE PLAY

PLAY AND CULTURE

The Spirit of Play

The Spirit of Adult Play

by Bonnie Neugebauer

Roger sits on the sofa with Carrie and Martha, age five, and asks: "Well, you girls must be about ready to get jobs! Have you found your own apartment yet?" Carrie and Martha eye him incredulously, then dissolve into giggles.

Delores joins Stephanie on the riding toy and together, adult and child, they whiz down the riding path, hair flying, smiles blazing.

Lynne and Keisha, age 25 or so, sit on the riverbank creating a miniature world with pine cones, rocks, and sticks. The focus of their bodies and their quiet, intense conversation exclude the rest of the campers.

Adults who play. They play with words and ideas. They use toys, invent props, appropriate resources for new purposes. They play with children and with other adults. They play because it is natural and because it makes them feel good. Children need these adults in their lives, people who will model the importance of play to living. But in so many early childhood programs, people have forgotten how to be playful. They are focused on order and routines, appearances and paperwork, agendas and lesson plans. There is no serendipity, no wonder, no surprise.

Some adults pplay naturally; they never forgot how. Other adults must relearn the joys of

"If I were to ask one thing above all others of teachers, it would be imagination . . . the kind of mind that is playful, fanciful, add in the relationships it perceives, that actively connects things as they are with things as they might be, that always pokes into corners and comes up with that which excites laughter or wonder."
Kenneth Eble, *The Perfect Education*

"We tend to be more adventurous at play because it feels safe. We stop evaluating ourselves. Play may be taken seriously, but it is the play and not ourselves that we are taking seriously — or else it is not really play at all."
Mindfulness, Ellen Langer

playfulness. But play is consuming, and adults and children who would play must be willing to spend freely, to squander, to waste (if you will), to be extravagant with their:

Time — Play must exist in the context of timelessness. The process is valued beyond the outcome of the play, so it must be possible to continue the experience across blocks of time, even across days and weeks. The play must find its own end, just as it found its own beginning.

Energy — Play requires total commitment. Players need to focus their attention on what they are doing without regard for what is happening elsewhere. There is no place for concern about the next activity or concurrent distractions. In play we are not afraid of what might prove difficult, or complex.

Resources — Play consumes resources. For a block city to grow there must be enough blocks to meet the ever expanding need. Castles require a beach to meet the ever expanding need. Paper sculptures require sufficient materials to rework ideas and fulfill projections.

Sense of Self — Play requires that one forget oneself. If self-conscious about their

Towards a More Playful Spirit

What would happen if:

. . . parents found me playing when they arrived at the center? What would I be doing?

. . . parents come *to* the center to play with their children? How can I make this happen?

. . . teachers were comfortable playing during the workday? Would it be okay to play alone or with other adults, or would it only be okay to play with children?

. . . I turned my most hateful task into play? How could I accomplish this?

. . . I didn't worry about making mistakes or failing? What if I didn't care about making a fool of myself?

. . . I did the things that I really enjoy frequently? What are those things in my life?

play, about how others will view either their play or the products of their play, children and adults are crippled. Their play is distorted by other consciousness.

Sense of Order — Play demands a certain amount of chaos. There must be room for using things and doing things in new ways. Play equipment and space must be flexible to meet the changing needs of the players. There must be storage for uncompleted play, and respect for unfinished spaces. Players require a degree of uncertainty and support for taking risks. Play is nurtured when there is no labeling of wrong and right.

Joy — Play without enjoyment is just plain hard work. Players need to laugh, and boast, and practice. There are many choices to be made, and each is a challenge. Play brings out the best in each of us.

It is often said that play is the work of children. What then, is the play of adults? For a fortunate few, work is play. But for far greater numbers of adults work is work; and there is not enough time for real, natural play. Or we are not sure enough of ourselves to take risks and to be spontaneous. What would happen if we approached everything in our lives with a more playful spirit? How would this playful spirit change our workday, our parenting, our lovemaking? With effort, the play of adults can be life.

"This is why play feels so good. Discovering and using the essence of any part of ourselves is the most euphoric experience of all. We were taught to say that play is the work of children. But watching and listening to them, I saw that play was nothing less than Truth and Life." VivianPaley, *the boy who would be a helicopter*

Bonnie Neugebauer is managing editor of *Exchange, The Early Childhood Leaders' Magazine Since 1978.*

The Play's the Thing:
Styles of Playfulness

by Elizabeth Jones

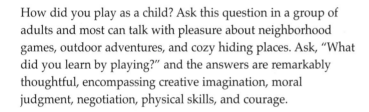

How did you play as a child? Ask this question in a group of adults and most can talk with pleasure about neighborhood games, outdoor adventures, and cozy hiding places. Ask, "What did you learn by playing?" and the answers are remarkably thoughtful, encompassing creative imagination, moral judgment, negotiation, physical skills, and courage.

Once when I asked these questions of a teaching staff, one teacher insisted that she *didn't* play as a child. There were knowing nods among her colleagues; a notorious workaholic and perfectionist, she was an inflexible thinker unable to compromise on program issues. "I'll bet there's a connection," one of them said thoughtfully. I'll bet there is, too.

The spontaneous play of young children is their highest achievement. In their play, children invent the world for themselves and create a place for themselves in it. They are re-creating their pasts and imagining their futures, while grounding themselves in the reality and fantasy of their lives here-and-now. (Jones & Reynolds, 1992, p. 129)

Children at play are constructing their individual identities as well as their knowledge of the world. The choosing child is saying, in effect, "This is who I am. This is what I want to do. This is what I need to do it with. When I play with others, I can negotiate with them to include my experiences as well as theirs. We talk about what we're doing, and we act it out. I need to keep playing until I'm done." (Jones, 1990, p. 11)

What's play? Choosing for oneself. Children need to play, and so do adults, especially those who spend much of their time with children. Working in child care, it's important that adults be able to make choices for themselves, inventing things they like to do, rather than simply implementing plans made by someone else. As any child can tell you, if someone else makes you do it, it's not play. Teachers, like children, are most competent when they're playing — that is, when they're staying alert to the action and the possibilities, choosing, planning, negotiation, and elaborating.

Play is invented by each player; imitation is not the same as play. Good teaching ideas often reflect a particular teacher's preferred play mode. In Vivian Paley's "storyplay" (1981), she invites children to dictate stories and later casts them to be enacted in the group. Linda Gibson, discovering that three year olds' fascination with the sound patterns of language matched her own (she was writing a dissertation on children's word-play), ended each morning in her preschool class with "Rhyme Time" (1989, pp. 53-54). My own children at home frequently re-created dramatic episodes from the stories I read to them:

"Little Girl, why for you move?" asks the Gunniwolf.

"I no move," she answers, trembling.

"Then you must sing me that guten sweeten song again," he growls.

"Kum-kwa, khi-wa," she sings, until her song puts him to sleep and she can run pitty pat home, hoping he won't come hunker-cha hunker-cha after her — and Michael as Gunniwolf pounced on his sister Suzanne time after time. She loved both the scariness and the power of her song (Little Girl always gets away). (Harper, 1967)

Teachers Mamie King, Maggie Pucillo, and Georgina Villarino are all imaginative friendly visitors when domestic play is in progress in the preschool sandbox or playhouse.

Girl, handling play phone to Mamie: "It's your mom."

Mamie, on phone: "Hello. How you doing? Did you pick up that hamburger meat for me? And could you pick up some taco sauce for me — and lettuce and tomatoes? I'd really appreciate it."

Child to Georgina, in the sand: "More cake?"

Georgina: "Okay, vanilla. No more chocolate."

Maggie, to child approaching playhouse: "Hi, sis! We're having a cheese sandwich. Jessica, the phone's for you. Who is it? Is that who you thought it would be?" Leaving: "Thank you, Richard. That was a very tasty snack."

I love building miniature worlds, on the floor with blocks and animals, or outdoors with rocks and sticks and leaves. I like animals better than vehicles, but either will do. My grandson Evan prefers vehicles; and one evening when he was rather aimlessly driving a trucks around the living room I was unable to resist joining in. We ended up with a newspaper-strip road taped to the floor, a Lego® garage, and several busy vehicles coming and going.

Doug Tolbert is a master inventor of large-scale play settings, improvising on the spot as he notices the play potential of available materials and the interests of four-year-old master players. Children watch and help with construction, and then Doug stands back to watch them play, occasionally helping as needed. One day the climbing structure became a boat with a bamboo mast (the child care yard is bordered by bamboo) and a parachute for a sail; the sail could be raised and lowered by two children working together. Another day a train was constructed out of several large packing boxes, a crate for the cow-catcher, a pot and mallet suspended from an overhead bamboo rod for the bell, ad a gallon plastic jug of flour, also suspended, for the smoke stack (when children blew through a tube in its bottom, *smoke* arose).

Adults need not join the play in order to acknowledge their admiration of it:

"Once upon a time," said Joan to her small class of three year olds, whom she had called into a snug circle as their going camping play was coming to an end, and before clean-up time, "there were one, two, three, four, five, six, seven, eight children who went camping together." "Me!" said Charlie excitedly. "Me, too!" said Alicia, echoed by others. "Yes, Charlie, and Alicia, and Mark went camping," acknowledged Joan, going on to name every child. "They put their sleeping bags in the car, and they put their tent in the car, and they put their food in the car . . . " (Jones & Reynolds, 1992, p. 125).

Joan gets particular pleasure from observing the details of children's dramatic play. Here she has used her observations to retell the story of their play to children, affirming their good ideas and encouraging them to "do it again." Her adult play — observing children — becomes a way to support their play.

Each of the adults mentioned above gets special pleasure from involving children in an activity she/he has invented for their delight *and* hers/his. In turn, part of the children's pleasure comes from the adult's enthusiasm. "Children, of course, sense what their teachers value and will move in the directions adult favor" (Gibson, 1989, p. 53). As teachers or parents, we are never neutral; by what we choose to acknowledge and participate in, we are communicating to children what we think is important. Fortunately, adults have diverse interests, and children learn different things from the different people in their lives.

It is important, however, that children learn that *they* are competent people with good ideas. They can be denied this right by adults whose need to play a starring role leads them to ignore the fact that play is the children's turf, which needs to be entered with care. Adults itching to play teacher are likely to interrupt children's play for the sake of their own wonderful ideas.

A simple arrangement of eight hairs in double rows in the corner of the three year old room has been stimulating bus play for several days. Today several boys have donned Batman apes. "I blue Batman, they orange Batmen," explains one. They are roaming the room, as are several girls in high heels. "Okay, Batman," says the teacher assistant. "What's Batman going to do today?" "Drive the bus," says one of the orange Batmen. They board the bus. A little later, as the assistant walks by, she observes: "Oh, you're driving the bus. Where's the bus going today?" "To school," the driver decides.

The lead teacher has put on a record and is clapping and dancing. She grabs the hands of a couple of girls as they high-heel by, and they dance with her. She organizes a parade with instruments.

Play flows around the room. From time to time there are half a dozen bus riders, some with babies. Orange Batman is heard asking, across the room, "Want to go with us on the bus?" Blue Batman: "I'm reading a book." "I leaving! I leaving!" calls the bus driver.

Lead teacher: "Okay. Five more minutes to clean-up; we're going outside and paint. Let's take off your Superman cape," she says to Batman. "Children who are very quiet can help carry the paint out."

The children, who have been playing for only half an hour, have shown no signs of readiness for a new activity. But the teacher, who loves to paint and has decorated the room with her creations, is happiest when she can be the star, and now she is eager for them to play *her* good idea. In contrast, her assistant, who has no wish to be the center of attention, has been quietly extending *children's* good ideas.

Play is children's world, and adults who take it over are denying children's need to invent it for themselves. Yet children benefit from adults' ideas, and adults benefit from being free to do things they like to do. That's how energy is created and sustained, and adults working in child care need all the energy they can find. For the most part, appropriate adult *play* in group

In Play, Children Learn . . .

To make appropriate choices among many possibilities.

To use their imagination, to improvise, to think flexibly, and explore new options.

To be aware of their own real interests, without being distracted by other possibilities: to say "yes" and to say "no."

To solve problems, both with materials and with people.

To cooperate with other children in the creation of mutually satisfying projects.

To work through their feelings in creative, non-destructive ways.

To pay attention to a project until it's done.

To use something — a dramatic action, a word, a toy, a set of blocks, a collection of marks on paper — to represent something else — a real experience, a powerful feeling. Practice in these sorts of representation is essential in the process of becoming literate, which is another form or representation.

To see themselves a competent and interesting people, with useful skills and good ideas.

---

programs takes place around the periphery of the children's action — in setting the stage, adding props and dramatic ideas, helping with problem-solving, observing and talking about children's good ideas, and inventing new plays based on those observations. It's a delicate balance, sustained primarily by observing children, observing oneself, and being open to questions from other observers in a continuing process of reflection and dialogue (Jones & Lakin, 1986; Carter & Jones, 1990; Jones & Carter, 1991).

Adults can learn to share their own playfulness with children without overwhelming them or performing for them, if they stay aware of children's developmental levels, children's interests, and what's playful for children.

References

Carter, M., & Jones, E. (September/October 1990). "The Teacher as Observer: The Director as Role Model." *Exchange, 75*, 27-30.

Gibson, L. (1989). *Literacy Learning in the Early Years: Through Children's Eyes*. New York: Teachers College Press.

Harper, W. (1967). *The Gunniwolf*. New York: E. P. Dutton.

Jones, E. (October 1990). "Playing Is My Job." *Thrust for Educational Leadership, 20*:2, 10-13.

Jones, E., & Carter, M. (January/February 1991). "Teachers as Scribe and Broadcaster: Using Observation to Communicate." *Exchange, 77*, 35-38.

Jones, E., & Lakin, M. B. (March 1986). "Reflections and Dialogue: Ways to Grow Staff." *Exchange, 48*, 3-6.

Jones, E., & Reynolds, G. (1992). *The Play's the Thing: Teachers' Roles in Children's Play*. New York: Teachers College Press.

Paley, V. G. (1981). *Wally's Stories*. Cambridge: Harvard University Press.

Elizabeth Jones is a faculty member in Human Development at Pacific Oaks College in Pasadena, California — and online, in the College's distance learning program. Her books on play are *Playing to Get Smart* (with Renatta Cooper), and *The Play's the Thing* and *Master Players* (with Gretchen Reynolds).

Just Wondering: Building Wonder Into the Environment

by Jim Greenman

"This world, after all our science and knowledge, is still a miracle; wonderful, inscrutable, magical, and more, to whosoever will think it."
Thomas Carlyle

Children come to us stuffed with wonder, eyes lit bright with projects. Their hands are eager to pull apart life's mysteries, their voices ready to shout out accomplishments, each echo adding shape to their being. The primal urge to investigate does not stop there. The mouths of young children are there to taste and chew the world around them (admittedly, not always a pretty picture). Children are native sensualists, sucking up experience with genetically programmed gusto. Enthusiasm and curiosity race through the veins of children unless clotted by the forms adults impose on their lives.

To wonder is to question, to imagine, and speculate on what is and what isn't. To be full of wonder is to approach life with openness, an eagerness to know and experience. When something is WONDERFUL, it is something we take delight in — better than good and on the road to awesome.

What sort of environments supports wonder and wonderful things and experience? Wonder is not hard to do; group living is hard to do, particularly with children. Group living leads to institutionalization, which drives wonder underground.

For most of us, the wonder of life easily drifts into the background; it is the province of artists and children to throw light into the shadows of daily life and enliven our sensibilities. Children naturally poke into the corners and cracks of dreary commonplace reality. WOULD YOU PLEASE PAY ATTENTION, LIFE IS HAPPENING HERE!, they tell us with their enthusiasms and their questions.

A classroom filled with wonder is not necessarily full of spectacle or rare and dramatic events or fancy equipment.

Wonder is more often found in a collection of small moments when reality crystallizes and experience heightens.

There are the "I did it!" moments of wonder. The powers of "me" produce a sense of wonder in all of us that fuels striding on into the world: genuine accomplishment, real responsibilities carried out well.

In one small center, five year olds are occasionally entrusted with the responsibility of answering the phone. In another, children as young as two years old trek to the kitchen as waiters for second helpings.

There are the "this world is amazing and mysterious" moments that come with the discovery of how life works — birth, death, growth, love — and the moments of discovery of "how things work and happen" — machines, gravity, physics. Perhaps best of all are those "ain't life grand" moments of pure pleasure or beauty.

from *Sometimes Life Is Not A Literacy Experience*
by Eugene Lesser

Tonight I sat on my back porch
and drank a bowl of
Campbell's chicken vegetable soup.
All that time watching the moon
and feeling absolutely great.

What kills wonder?

Wonder is easily diminished in children's programs by:

The weight and volume of daily life in groups. The energy it takes children to fit in, to carve out relationships and zones of privacy, and to take care of the mechanics of life may force wonder into the shadows. Group life often rations wonder by imposing restrictions (no "running feet," "outside voices," "keep it clean," "wait your turn") that flatten experience to keep the forces of chaos as bay.

The unbearable lightness of cuteness. Cuteness robs wonder of its evocative power, pasteurizing awe and delight into one dimensional chuckles and fuzzy glows.

Seriousness. Early childhood is far too serious to take seriously — that is, the seriousness that leads to earnest and passionate discussion on "Johnny's motivation," or two pages devoted to peek-a-boo in an infant curriculum, or a Ph.D. thesis on the developmental progression of skills involved with using scissors. Wonder often invokes the imperative to be silly, in both children and adults. Silliness in turn knocks down the formal structures that sometimes hold too rigid the shape of our straight and narrow orientation to task and routine and self-importance. Without periodic silliness, life becomes dreary and inspiration dims.

Blandness and lack of standards. Experience is not equal. In decidedly un-wonderful programs, one gets the feeling that "a book is a book is a book," "a record is a record is a record," something taken from the shelf without much thought or enthusiasm. There is no sense of quality, of connection to the moment and the participants: that what is being heard or read has value and evocative power right now. One might hear Raffi in the background calling for movement as children, bemused and immobilized, sit at a table waiting for lunch, that album chosen because it was there. Or a listless reading of a long Disney Golden Book, a book with pictures too small to engage the increasingly restive large group. The joy of language and music fades in instances like this.

Gratuitous or unsought instruction. I watched as a mother and her four year old shared a moment at the zoo:

"Look, Johnny, flamingos!" the mother exclaimed. "What are they?"

"Birds," said Johnny.

"What color are they?"

"Pink," said Johnny.

"How many are there?"

"Three," said Johnny.

Two giraffes lumbered into view. Before Johnny's determined mom could open her mouth, Johnny called out: "Giraffes, yellow, two." Johnny had overdosed on teachable moments.

Wonder comes from a child's search and discovery, not from our dutiful prodding.

False engagement. Falsity diminishes wonder, and false engagement is probably worse than no engagement at all. An environment of "that's nice (pretty, good)" diminishes the child quest.

Egocentrism, fatigue, and stress (ours). Teachers are egocentric the minute they focus on teaching (not learning) and caring (not care). Teacher fatigue and stress leaves little energy for real engagement with children.

Unbridled tidiness. Group living requires order, but an excess of tidiness sweeps life into narrow bins and tiny corners.

Disorder and chaos. Chaos is scary and makes us insecure. We withdraw. Clarity is lost when chaos rules, and choices become random, beauty a blur. Without order, wonder is submerged and goes unrecognized.

Fear. In many programs, there is a low-level current of fear that bumps and bruises, strains and tears will lead to recriminations against the staff. Fear of risk, challenge, and mess suffocates wonder. Safety is a real issue, but often blown to grotesque proportions by fear of liability in a litigious society that refuses to see that "accidents happen." Parents' real concerns about wear and tear on children and clothes is lessened din programs where mutual respect between parents and staff leads to discussions on how best to create a sensible environment of wonder an discovery.

Censorship and political correctness. Wonder is diluted by political correctness of all stripes. Yes, all sorts of behavior are not acceptable and have to be sanctioned, because they hurt others or create problems in group life. But to wonder is to imagine and pretend, to explore the world of "what if," a world that includes cross dressing, the immense power of imaginary weapons, and witches and monsters.

Tales of wonder

Five-year-old Anita and I were discussing wonderful things. We had rounded up the usual suspects of puppies and chocolate, puddles and Grandma's house, fishing with Dad, and riding her bike. Getting ready to go, Anita looked at me shyly and (slyly) and said, "and, you know, there's always poop." Take your epiphanies as they come.

Environments that support wonder

There is no mystery here. Wonder thrives in environments that embrace childhood and support the adults that live and work with them.

Furniture and Equipment to Promote Wonder

The Miracle of Life:

Incubators
Bird cages
Aquariums
Animal cages
Ant farms
Butterfly gardens
Bird feeders and bird baths
Baby carriers and furniture that creates laps
    (heartbeats and human contact)
Magnifying glasses

Alchemy and Chemistry:

Sinks
Plastic tubs
Water tables
Electric skillets
Microscopes
Toilets (unauthorized)

The Magic of Cause and Effect:

Motors
Fans
Pulleys, levels, block and tackle
Computers

The Magic of Vision:

Lamps
Flashlights
Prisms
Stained glass
Canopies
Mobiles, hangings

The Wonder of Language:

Tape recorders and headphones
Good books that value art and language
Typewriters
Computers

The Joy of Invented Places:

Blocks of all kinds, and more blocks
Planks
Mirrors
Connectors of all kinds — tape, string, nails, paste, glue

The Wonder of Caring Adults:

Adult furniture and the support to create good places
Ample storage

A child seeking active exploration would ask of a place:

- Can I be messy?
- Can I be alone?
- Can I move?
- Can I be outside — a lot?
- Can I spread out over space and time?
- Can I be noisy?
- Can I get some quiet?
- Can I be still?
- Can I do MY thing?
- Where's the stuff, the loose parts: the raw material of discovery?

A teacher might ask:

- Is there enough room?
- Can we keep it clean?
- Is there a place for me?
- Is there enough storage?
- Can we keep it safe?
- Will I get the support of staff and parents?

Remembrance of things past: A cautionary tale

One can get carried away with the romance of childhood and forget that children are quickly acculturated. They, too, live in the real world — like it or not — the world of miracle, wonder, Macys, and Madonna. When my daughter Emma was four, we spent a day together that I remember with intoxicating clarity — a warm summer day of picking wildflowers amid clouds of butterflies, paddling down a creek past baby ducks and egrets, and later being enveloped by grandparental pride. When I asked her about this day of wonder years later, she remembered it well. "Oh yeah, that's when I got my new red two piece bathing suit." Proust would have kicked her. The moral here is not to diminish the importance of the natural world, only to note that a new red two-piece bathing suit is a pretty wonderful thing, too.

Resources for wonder

InsectLore
PO Box 1535
Shafter, CA 93263
(800) LIVEBUG (548-3284) • www.insectlore.com
A unique company that sells butterflies, tadpoles, and all sorts of science-nature products.

Edmund Scientific
60 Pearce Avenue
Tonawanda, NY 14150
(800) 728-6999 • www.scientificsonline.com
All sorts of science and discovery equipment.

Bear Blocks
1132 School Street
Mansfield, MA 02048
(800) 424-2327
Carpeted planks and blocks to create ever-changing spaces.

Fancy Foote-Works
549 Moscow Road
Hamlin, NY 14464
(716) 964-8260
Custom built environments, lifts, and play equipment.

How Wonderful is Your Classroom?

Walk into a child's place and create a sensory snapshot. Check with a + or – what you find.

The Smell of Wonder

___ Flowers and plants
___ Baking
___ Herbs and spices

Subtract if your smell:

___ Disinfectant

The Sounds of Wonder

___ Child laughter
___ Adult laughter
___ Silly voices
___ The sounds of birds, animals, fish tanks
___ Rapt silence
___ Music that creates a mood or sets bodies in motion
___ "Wow," "I love it," "Look, look," "I did it"

The Touch of Wonder

___ Natural materials: wood, stone, and grass
___ Sand, water, mud, clay
___ Slimy, slippery, squishy, squeezy things

___ Fragile things that require gentleness
___ Laps and hugs

Subtract if nearly all you touch is:

___ Plastic, Formica®, polyurethane, or metal

The Sights of Wonder

___ Smiles on children's faces
___ Smiles on adult's faces
___ Looks of intense concentration
___ "Faraway" dreamy looks of cabbages and kings
___ "I did it" grins, maniacal grins of pleasure
___ Living things — plants, animals, birds, fish
___ Beautiful things — respectfully displayed

Subtract if you see:

___ Vacant stares
___ Commercial images and an abundance of "cute"

Which of these words apply to your classroom?

___ Astonishment
___ Lovely
___ Sight to behold
___ Mysterious

Jim Greenman is Senior Vice President for Education and Program Development at Bright Horizons Family Solutions. Bright Horizons has over 650 centers and schools in the United States, the United Kingdom, Canada, and Ireland. Jim has over 30 years' experience as an educator and early childhood administrator. His experience ranges from working with employer-sponsored child care to inner city, hospital, and university programs; early childhood and family education programs; Head Start, family child care, and public and private schools. Jim has played a significant role in the facility and program design process for over 100 early childhood projects and teaches the Institute on Child Care Design at the Harvard Graduate School of Design. His numerous books, articles, and videos include *Caring Spaces/Learning Places: Children's Environment that Work* (Exchange Press) and *Prime Times: A Handbook for Excellence in Infant and Toddler Care* (Redleaf Press). He received a Master's Degree and completed additional advanced graduate studies at the University of California at Berkeley.

THE SPIRIT OF PLAY

Catching the Spirit: Training Teachers to Be Playful

by Margie Carter

As an adult college student earnestly preparing myself to teach young children, it never occurred to me that I was unlearning a basic element of successful early childhood education — immersion in play. I was *very* serious about being a *good* teacher: teaching children the skills they need to be successful, helping them with problems, sharing their values and attitudes toward responsible adulthood.

What influenced my return to the delight of play was not my teacher education program, but a friendship with two gay men. On Friday nights they coaxed this serious college student out of the library and into a mountain of leaves gathered on the October campus. Games of charades, theme dinners, the trips to the store in costumes soon lightened my step, loosened my laughter, and imbued me with a new sense of inquisitiveness about the world. I even went to register for a physics class.

Some 30 years later, I find myself drawing on these memories as I come across teachers who are misguided in their understandings of "school readiness." Seeing little time provided for open-ended exploration in their classrooms and "free time" viewed as the transition spaces between the real curriculum, I wonder if these teachers, too have unlearned the importance of play in their lives.

Helping teachers identify their own experiences and attitudes toward play

Some teachers are aware that play is missing from their lives, while others don't recognize the absence. Many equate play with entertainment or recreational sports. It's helpful to clarify our terms, and there are numerous books on children's play to draw upon. In the foreword to *The Play's the Thing* by Jones and Reynolds, Liz Prescott quotes one of my favorite definitions of play — a "bubble of illusion." This, in combination with the authors' defining of play as "autonomous choice of activity," can serve as a reference for teacher exploration of play in their lives.

■ **Strategy — Share a story.** Have teachers talk in pairs, remembering a favorite play experience from their childhoods. Then ask them to share a story of play in their adult life. Follow with a group discussion on emerging common elements among their stories of childhood play, comparing and contrasting these to their adult play stories. What prompted this play? Did other children or adults have a role in it? Were any expectations, inventions, or conventions explored?

■ **Strategy — Time with loose parts.** In the Beginnings Workshop on Creativity and Learning (May/June 1992, *Exchange*), the articles both Walter Drew and I contributed describe workshop experiences for adults which provide them with a large supply of simple materials to play with uninterrupted for an extended period of time. Stress the importance of playing as adults in these activities, rather than pretending to be children. The exploration, sorting, building, and creating can relax adults into a rediscovering of the value of play; and the follow-up discussion can focus attention on the elements that kept them engaged, as well as the knowledge and skill that is learned through extended play. Teachers may want to try this activity with parents as a way to communicate the value of play and its relationship to the learning process.

Helping teachers pay attention to children's play

When children are independently involved in play, it often goes unnoticed by teachers who use this time for other pressing needs in their job — recordkeeping; housekeeping; resource gathering and filing; consultation with a co-worker, parent, or supervisor. Yet observation of children at play is sure to bring teachers delight as well as insight. It is invaluable for their ongoing curriculum planning conversations with child and parent, and their own growth and sustenance in this undervalued, underpaid profession.

■ **Strategy — Observing for the kinds of play.** To help teachers understand and support children's play, Deb Curtis and I frequently structure what Jones calls a "closed means — open ends" training activity. We put teachers into small groups and ask them to each choose to assume the role of player or observer. Each group is given a set of open-ended materials and, while the observers take notes, the players are given a sequence of instructions (unknown to the observers) to be done for about five minutes each.

Round #1: Players nonverbally explore the materials as if they have never seen them before. Explore with your senses and discover the attributes of the materials. Arrange, manipulate, or transform the materials in any way that helps you get to know them, but don't make anything with them.

Round #2: Players explore what they can make with the materials, verbally or nonverbally.

Round #3: Players use the materials as props in dramatic play they create together, assuming roles and talking with each other.

Round #4: Players use the materials and play a made-up game with rules that get created as they go along.

This activity generates understandings about the stages of children's play and a productive discussion about adult interactions that disrupt or keep the play going. Concise related reading can be found in Chapter 1 of Jones' and Reynolds', *The Play's the Thing,* and Hohmann's article, "How to Observe Children at Work Time," in the *High/Scope Resource,* Fall 1991.

■ **Strategy — Observing children with focused questions.** Ask teachers to answer these questions as they observe a child in the classroom or on videotape:

Describe what you specifically saw.

How would you name the essence of the child's play during this time?

What does this child know how to do?

What does this child find frustrating?

How does this child feel about her or himself?

What might this child need to continue this play?

Creating playful activities for training on any topic

It's hard to genuinely value play for children if we as adults don't have it in our own lives. At the heart of my planning for any inservice workshop are the questions "How can I set up playful ways for the adults to explore this topic? What experiences will not only deepen their understandings, but renew their spirits and desire to play?" Teachers already valuing a play curriculum also find playful training activities useful as this enhances their ability to articulate the significance of play to parents who are pressing for more academics in their young child's day.

■ **Strategy — Turn reading material into a sorting activity.** Reading and applying what one has read is a difficult task for many teachers who are exhausted at the end of te work day and must focus on family and other tasks in the evening. Certain articles lend themselves to photo enlarging and cutting into a sorting game. The *Developmentally Appropriate Practice* book by Sue Bredekamp works well for this, sorting practices into "appropriate" and "inappropriate" columns. Much of the writing by Diane Trister Dodge, including her articles in past issues of *Exchange,* her book, *The Creative Curriculum for Early Childhood,* and its trainer's guide, also features charts with columns suitable for sorting and classifying our teaching practices. Dodge's *A Parent's Guide to Early Childhood Education* has a section with columns of "When Children Do This: — They Are Learning To:" which teachers, in turn, can use as an activity to help parents see the learning inherent in children's play.

■ **Strategy — Turn early childhood education concepts into diverse representations.** Have small groups discuss handouts and create a representation of the ideas for the others to see and discuss. I've done t his with sections of NAEYC accreditation criteria and seen remarkably creative drawings, block constructions, pantomimes, and human sculptures created to portray interpretations of these ideas in practice.

My colleague, Joan Newcomb, gives teachers a stack of newspaper and masking tape with the task of building an environment related to the topic at hand — a space that they would like to play in, one that reflects their home or culture, a place that would appeal to toddlers, and so on.

Training teachers to be playful involves providing opportunities to reflect on play in their own lives, enhancing their desire and ability to pay attention to children's play, and having playful activities to explore any inservice topic. A final warning: planning with these guidelines may spark a renewed playfulness in a frazzled director's life. There have been reported sightings of child care directors n piles of October leaves and in outrageous hats of newspaper, baubles, and feathers at supermarket check-out stands during the dreary winter months.

Margie Carter teaches community college classes and travels widely to consult and speak. She is the producer of numerous staff development videos and co-author of six early childhood books, including *Training Teachers: A Harvest of Theory and Practice, The Art of Awareness, Side by Side: Mentoring Teachers for Reflective Practice,* and *Designs for Living and Learning.* Margie believes that teachers should be educated in ways that parallel what we want them to do with children. Active in the Worthy Wage Campaign, Margie is stubbornly passionate about issues of peace and justice.

The Value of Play

THE VALUE OF PLAY

Play, Policy, and Practice: The Essential Connections

by Edgar Klugman and Sandra Waite-Stupiansky

Three children are deeply engaged in a blockbuilding project, two researchers are discussing teacher entry into child play, an educator is preparing an article on the value of play as it occurs in an early childhood program. Are all these people — their thoughts, ideas and work — connected? We strongly argue "Yes" — in fact, the connections made among and between these people are crucial to quality care and education of young children.

Have parents ever confronted you, the director, about providing more academic programming? Have you interacted with teachers who want to integrate play into the curriculum but aren't sure how? Have teachers in your program read about research on the importance of play for later learning? Interactions such as these point to the necessity for finding, making, and supporting connections among play, policy, and practice.

The National Association for the Education of Young Children, in its publication, *Developmentally Appropriate Practice in Early Childhood Programs* (Bredekamp & Copple, 1997) takes the stand that play belongs at the center of a curriculum designed for the young child. As a matter of fact, ongoing research, as well as publication after publication in the early childhood field, emphasizes the crucial, intrinsic connections among play, policy, and practice.

Over the last century, research and theory in early childhood education have continued to point to the connections between play and learning. Theories and research findings of Dewey, Piaget, and Vygotsky first informed educators of the active role children take in their learning. More recently, the curriculum model of the Reggio Emilia schools in Italy demonstrates that children act as the inventors and constructors of their own knowledge through their active and interactive explorations of the world. In the words of Loris Malaguzzi (1993), the teacher-

theorist whose ideas shaped the schools in Reggio Emilia, "Always and everywhere children take an active role in the construction and acquisition of learning and understanding" (p. 60). If educators, parents, administrators, and others responsible for young children accept children as active learners, then play becomes a vehicle, we would argue the most important vehicle, to empower children as learners.

In a work-oriented culture, such as ours, play is often perceived as the inverse of productive work. Play is reserved for after school or after work. It is often seen as the frivolous activity that children and adults earn through their hard work.

Yet, the widely-accepted definition of play in early childhood literature focuses on the intrinsically-motivated, child-directed, open-ended nature of play. Play is exploratory and process-oriented more than product-driven (Waite-Stupiansky, 1997). Play and learning are inextricably intertwined for young children. In fact, a recent study by Cooney (1997) found that preschool-age children blur the lines between play and work. It is not until formal schooling that children begin to differentiate between the two activities. Thus, play and work are not dichotomous, but are part of the whole-thinking-learning process for young children.

As directors/policy makers, we are presented with a special leadership role in facilitating and helping to encourage the dialogue around play, policy, and practice and in affecting the perceptions and decisions which relate to it. Only to the extent that we can do this can we affect the quality of experiences offered to the children in our programs. We need to find ways to welcome and integrate the voices of children, classroom teachers, parents, researchers, teacher educators, administrators, and policy makers, each of whom represents an important perspective on the issues surrounding children's play.

Sylvia Washington, a new director of a small child care center, finds that the teaching staff are most comfortable using play materials which are highly structured, such as coloring books, puzzles, and other *quiet materials*, leaving little opportunity for children to use their own ideas, imaginations, or creativity. They leave the children completely on their own and spend the outdoor time talking to each other. The educational background of the teaching staff includes a high school diploma for all, and some additional college courses in the liberal arts and general education for two. One staff member received a bachelor's degree in English. The Center director has a master's degree in leadership and early childhood education.

Since the director feels strongly that play is one of the most important components of the program, and since she is new to the setting, she uses her entry process to dialogue with individuals who are directly or indirectly involved with the program. She sets up meetings with teachers, board members, and parents. She invites their thoughts about the school, the overall program, and children's play in particular. She develops a few questions to ask all constituents so that feedback about the findings can be provided to members of each of the groups being interviewed. Interestingly, she finds that the teachers all rate play as theoretically the most important activity in the center. The parents are most concerned that the children "learn something." Board members see learning and play as important dimensions of the program, but add safety as their additional concern.

As a next step, the director invites each group to meet with her to share feedback on the findings and to begin to point out ways to address the concerns and issues raised by each constituency. The meetings focus simultaneously on ways to address the safety of children, their play, and their learnings. The teaching staff decides to focus the year's staff development effort on play and learning. The board requests that a joint subcommittee be set up to consider the three issues of play, learning, and safety, with representation from all three constituencies. The director sees that it would be helpful if a parent and a board member were to become a link between the sub-committee and the staff development sessions. While this seems somewhat difficult in terms of time arrangements, two people from each category volunteer to alternately attend the teaching staff development seminars.

Since the concern of all constituent groups is children's learning, the first few sessions of the staff development seminar focus on play and learning. The director suggests that each person think about her own childhood play memories. To help people get started, the director suggests that it might be useful to think about any of the following: a) the age of the player at the time of the play memory; b) the place in which the play memory occurred (e.g., was it indoors or outdoors? school or home?); c) whether the memories were of playing alone or with others;

if with others, who they were; d) the toys, play equipment, or natural materials such as wood, sand, or water, involved in the play memory. Now the group of teachers and representatives from the board and parents analyze their childhood play memories from a learning perspective. As they go through the process, the extent of interdependence and intertwining of play and learning becomes clearer. The teachers, board members, and the parents are astonished at this interconnection. The next sessions are planned to focus on classroom observation, assessment of play, and a new look at the role of the adult as teacher, facilitator, and life-span-expander for children.

Needless to say, those involved in this integrated process are able to gain a new level of understanding and respect for children's play. At a later point in the year, when it is time to plan the following year's budget, board members who have experienced the integrated staff development sessions will have far better grounding in what it can mean for program and children when integrated, carefully designed staff development seminars, such as those offered by Sylvia, are made available. The board easily passes the necessary separate budget items to support the ongoing seminars and begins to accrue for the center carefully selected, play-enhancing materials and equipment for the next academic year. This center is well on its way toward the goals of staff development, board development, and program development and improvement. A *fall-out* product is the team building among the diverse constituent groups which undoubtedly will continue to be very useful during the following year as new challenges are encountered and met.

To return to the initial question: Are there essential connections among play, policy, and practice? This example illustrates that there are powerful and positive connections in programs that value play as the vehicle for learning. The constituents involved in the preceding example would give a resounding affirmative response. They can refer to the work they have done and its many positive results, to explain why the connections are crucial. In the process, they revisited the play experiences they had as children and discovered the reasons why play and learning cannot be separate for young children.

References

Bradekamp, S., & Copple, C. (editors). (1997). *Developmentally appropriate practice in early childhood programs* (revised edition). Washington, DC: NAEYC.

Cooney, M. (1997). "Play from a child's perspective." *Play, Policy, and Practice Connections,* the Newsletter of the Play, Policy, and Practice Caucus of the National Association for the Education of Young Children. (Available by writing Sandra Waite-Stupiansky, Miller Research Learning Center, Edinboro University of PA, Edinboro, PA 16444).

Malaguzzi, L. (1993). "History, ideas and basic philosophy: An interview with Lella Gandini." In C. Edwards, L. Gandini, and G. Forman (editors). *The hundred languages of children: The Reggio Emilia approach to early childhood education.* Norwood, NJ: Ablex Publishing Corp.

Waite-Stupiansky, S. (1997). *Building understanding together: A constructivist approach to early childhood education.* Albany, NY: Delmar Publishers.

Sandra Waite-Stupiansky, Ph.D. teaches preschoolers and kindergartners at the Miller Research Learning Center on the campus of Edinboro University of Pennsylvania. Her book, *Building Understanding Together: A Constructivist Approach to Early Childhood Education,* was published by Delmar Publishers (Albany, NY). She serves as the Managing Editor for the *Play, Policy, and Practice Connections* newsletter.

Edgar Klugman, Ed.D. is a specialist in child and family policy. He is one of the founders of the Play, Policy and Practice Caucus and consulting editor of *Play, Policy and Practice Connections* newsletter. He has co-authored and edited *Children, Families & Government,* Cambridge University Press; *Children's Play and Learning: Perspectives and Policy Implications,* Teachers College Press; and *Play, Policy and Practice,* Redleaf Press.

THE VALUE OF PLAY

What's New in Play Research?

by Doris Pronin Fromberg

Everybody is an expert in identifying when young children are at play, because we can see it happening, and we expect that children will play. We are less ready to consider that some of the same processes go underground throughout adult life. By looking at what play is, what children do while they engage in play, and what benefits they derive from play, we have a chance to learn how they think and what they know. Sociodramatic play is a powerful developmental activity and form of assessment.

Defining and describing play processes

Play is symbolic (acting "as if" or "what if"), meaningful, active, pleasurable even when serious, voluntary and intrinsically motivated, rule-governed (implicitly or explicitly), and episodic (shifting spontaneously and flexibly). The philosopher John Dewey (1933) suggests a continuum of fooling . . . play . . . work . . . drudgery, and indicates that a **balance** between play and work is the reasonable place for education to take place. Psychologist Lev Vygotsky (1978) sees play as a rule-bound form of impulse control that leads children's underlying representational development. He sees play as a "scaffolding" that takes place as children engage in social activity at the edge of their learning potential ("zone of proximal development"). When children play, they are able to leave the play framework, communicate with one another about how to play (e.g., "You be the doctor and I'll be the sick baby"), and reenter the play (e.g., "Waah!") after having negotiated the rules of engagement.

Script building[29] together is the powerful, central process in sociodramatic play. Children use their personal and cultural knowledge of events (e.g., shopping, cooking, weddings, street scenes, television settings) to build scripts together. Using the outline of their daily life experiences, children create new scripts "through shared predictability and collaborative novelty".[22] They learn a great deal about what other people understand by their reactions to suggestions, come to understand other children's perspectives, and refine their ways to influence others' rules in the script. In these ways, script building is similar to the relationships of an editor and author or coach and player.

Theory of mind researchers[1,3] try to understand how children represent the real as well as the imaginary, think about their own thinking, and the thinking of others. They have asked children about desires, beliefs, false beliefs, and deception as well as looked at children's play. The active verbal and physical nature of sociodramatic play offers opportunities for such study. There is a sense from both script theory and theory of mind study that human beings, through social interaction, develop the use of multiple "mental models"[18] and "image schemas"[23] to represent their experiences. In these ways, play functions with a "grammar" of experience in which its surface forms represent underlying integrated processes.

Play and development

There is agreement among researchers that engaging in sociodramatic play helps children to develop their literacy skills, social competence, and their cognitive ability, especially problem solving. There is also a group of studies, that have been challenged, which have found that children's pretend play improves their imagination and creativity.

Literacy skills develop through opportunities for social interaction. A body of applied research points to the importance of simultaneously varying props, writing materials, and play themes in order to enrich children's literacy, for example, when children play with beauty parlor, post office, bank, and hospital props that include language literacy materials[6] and emergent numeracy[7] materials. Other studies have found that children's story recall improves when they have engaged in role playing after hearing a story,[26] particularly when small groups had opportunities to play out the stories.[35]

Social competence appears to be more apparent in pretend play than other activities[2] and children maintain stability and consistency by sharing meanings. Children's play with older children, siblings, and parents is more advanced and extended than with peers.[20] "Master players"[28] are more flexible, fluid, cooperative, and engaged in extended play. More secure children show similar characteristics.[13] These characteristics make it easier for other children to accept them and their ideas. On the other hand, children who have had many different group settings are less competent in their play.[19]

Cognitive development takes place during pretend play. When teachers or parents have intervened by playfully modeling, providing varied props, and raising play-related questions, young children have become more flexible planners, used more expanded language, and sustained play for longer periods of time.[4, 11, 31] Researchers have found a relationship between enriched adult play intervention and children's academic skills, as well as I.Q.[21] with an improvement in systematic and process-oriented problem solving.[33] There is also evidence that the use of low-specificity toys is related to more interactive play and a longer shared play script.[24, 25]

Imagination helps when children need to wait because they create imaginary stories, and use analogies.[30] After exposure to modeling and the use of divergent materials, young children have been able to engage in more combinatorial play and make new connections.[9, 15, 26] Children seem to stimulate each other's imaginations when in groups of two or three, and working with the group itself might help to reduce aggressive behavior.[14] Methodological criticism of some of these studies, however, has become part of an ongoing dialogue.[9, 12, 32]

Integration of cognitive, linguistic, socioemotional, and creative processes characterizes pretend play. Problem solving, which children practice during their play, requires such integration. It is helpful to consider the integrative function of play as having lymphatic function within children's experience and learning. It is worthwhile, therefore, for teachers to provide opportunities for children to have the choice of a rich socio-dramatic play life in group settings.

Implications for teachers and administrators

Planning for sociodramatic play means providing time, space, resources, and support. Children need long blocks of time (a minimum of 45-60 minutes) in order to organize and play out their scripts. They need space with changing themes and props (4-6 weeks for a theme and related props). Maintaining the housekeeping center for the entire year as a housekeeping center reduces opportunities for expanded language and ideas to develop.[5] Extending opportunities for richly varied and novel experiences also adds to children's event knowledge, which forms the basis for their scripting of plays.

When teachers sit in the blocks area, a source of visual-spatial learnings that assist the development of children's mathematical competence,[22] more girls, who tend to remain near the teacher, are likely to participate. Literacy materials can be in the blocks area as well as other thematic sociodramatic play areas, including the housekeeping area. These provisions should be available among the choices in general activity periods during which small groups of children work together. Consider also the power of interage grouping for scaffolding children's play and learning. Teachers circulate and intervene unobtrusively.

It is relevant for teachers of young children to review their schedules in order to provide for mostly small groups to work together much of the time for longer time blocks. These provisions mean reviewing the daily schedule to eliminate many shorter time blocks and their related transition times, which denote more whole group instruction.

Questioning with a view toward expanding children's language use differs from questioning that demands a single correct answer. If there is only one answer and the teacher already knows it, then it is a testing or guessing exercise and not an authentic question. Children are able to expand their language use when teachers use open-ended questions to which children may respond with their ideas, opinions, preferences, or descriptions. Children can interpret and predict what might happen in a story and then role play different endings. When a teacher models divergent questioning and role playing, children learn to use a wider range of options in their pretend play and language use. Most important, children feel a sense of competence and power to choose. Such a sense of success goes a long way toward preventing the development of destructive behavior.

Ethical Teaching. Young children are often willing to please adults and can do many things that are not necessarily most helpful to their long-term development as responsible, independent, flexible, and socially competent thinkers. Parents sometimes have other ideas about what their children's school experience should look like. It helps, therefore, to document what children **are** learning, through photographs and slides, children's drawings and writings, language experience charts, one- or two-line notes home to each family on a rotating basis with information about what their child accomplished that day, and a newsletter describing the themes, books, and experiences to which children were exposed.

Adults who work with young children have an ethical responsibility to provide worthwhile experiences that can help young children feel successful as they construct many ways to work, play, and think. While sociodramatic play may be a vehicle for extending children's learning, it is worthwhile in its own right as a potentially empowering, integrative, joyful, aesthetic, and humanizing experience. The teacher whose focus and trust rest with children's construction of important integrated connections serves the ethical purpose of education. A sense of appreciation, respect, humor, and playfulness helps, too.

References

1 Astington, J. W. (1993). *The child's discovery of the mind.* Cambridge, MA: Harvard University Press.

2 Barnes, M. K., & Vangelisti, A. L. (1995). "Speaking in a double-voice: Role-making as influence in preschoolers' fantasy play situations." *Research on Language and Social Interaction, 28,* (4), 351-389.

3 Bartsch, K., & Wellman, H. M. (1995). *Children talk about the mind.* New York: Oxford University Press.

4 Bretherton, I., O'Connell, B., Shore, C., & Bates, E. (1984). "The effect of contextual variation on symbolic play development from 20 to 28 months." In I. Bretherton (editor), *Symbolic play: The development of social understanding* (pp. 271-298). New York: Academic Press.

5 Cazden, C. (1971). "Language programs for young children: Notes from England and Wales." In C. S. Lavatelli (editor), *Language training in early childhood education* (pp. 119-153). Urbana, IL: ERIC.

6 Christie, J. F. (editor). (1991). *Play and early literacy development.* Albany, NY: State University of New York Press.

7 Cook, D. (1996). "Mathematical sense making and role playing in the nursery." *Early Child Development and Care, 121,* 55-66.

8 Dansky, J. L. (1985). "Questioning 'A Paradigm Questioned': A commentary on Simon and Smith." *Merrill-Palmer Quarterly, 31,* 279-384.

9 Dansky, J. L. (1986). "Play and creativity in young children." In K. Blanchard, W. W. Anderson, G. E. Chick, and E. P. Johnson (editors), *The many faces of play* (pp. 69-79). Champaign, IL: Human Kinetics.

10 Dewey, J. (1933). *How we think.* Boston: Heath.

11 Dias, M. G., & Harris , P. L. (1988). "The effect of make-believe play on deductive reasoning." *Developmental Psychology 6,* 207-221.

12 Dunn, L., & Herwig , J. E. (1992). "Play behavior and convergent and divergent thinking skills of young children attending full-day preschool." *Child Study Journal, 22,* (1), 23-38.

13 Fagot, B. I. (1997). "Attachment, parenting, and peer interactions of toddler children." *Developmental Psychology, 33,* (3), 489-499.

14 Farver, J. (1996). "Aggressive behavior in preschoolers' social networks." *Early Childhood Research Quarterly, 11* (3), 333-350.

15 Feitelson, D., & Ross , G.S. (1973). "The neglected actor — play." *Human Development, 16,* 202-223.

16 Fromberg, D. P. (1998). "Play issues in early childhood education." In C. Seefeldt (editor), *Continuing issues in early childhood education* 2nd. edition. Columbus, OH: Merrill Macmillan.

17 Fromberg, D. P. (1992). "A review of research on play." In C. Seefeldt (editor), *The early childhood curriculum: A review of current research 3rd edition.* New York: Teachers College Press.

18 Harris, P. L., & Kavanaugh , R. D. (1993). "Young children's understanding of pretense." *Monographs of the Society for Research in Child Development, Serial No. 231, 58,* (1).

19 Howes, C., & Stewart , P. (1987). "Child's play with adults, toys, and peers: an examination of family and child-care influences." *Developmental Psychology, 23* (3), 423-430.

20 Howes, C. with Unger, O., & Matheson, C. C. (1992). *The collaborative construction of pretend: Social pretend play function.* Albany: State University of New York Press.

21 Levenstein, P. (1992). "Mother-child home program (Toy demonstrators).{ In L.R. Williams and D.P. Fromberg (editors), *The encyclopedia of early childhood education,* (pp. 481-482). New York: Garland.

22 Maccoby, E. E., & Jacklin , C. T. (1974). *The psychology of sex differences.* Stanford, CA: Stanford University Press.

23 Mandler, J.M. (1992). "How to build a baby: II. Conceptual primitives." *Psychological Review, 99,* (4), 587-604.

24 McGhee, P. E., Etheridge , L., & Berg , N.A. (1984). "Effect of toy structure on preschool children's pretend play." *Journal of Catholic Education, 144,* 209-217.

25 McLloyd, V. (1983). "The effects of the structure of play objects on the pretend play of low-income preschool children." *Child Development, 54,* 626-635.

26 Pellegrini, A. D. (1984). "The effects of exploration and play in young children's associative fluency. A review and extension

of training studies." In T.D. Yawkey and A.D. Pellegrini (editors), *Child's play: Developmental and applied* (pp. 237-253). Hillsdale, NJ: Lawrence Erlbaum.

27 Pellegrini, A. D. & Galda, L. (1982). "The effects of thematic-fantasy play training on the development of children's story comprehension." *American Education Research Journal, 19,* 443-452.

28 Reynolds, G, & Jones , E. (1997). *Master players.* New York: Teachers College Press.

29 Schank, R., & Abelson, R. (1977). *Scripts, plans, goals and understanding: An inquiry into human knowledge.* Hillsdale, NJ: Lawrence Erlbaum.

30 Singer, J. L., & Singer, D. (1979). "The values of imagination." In B. Suttonsmith (editor), *Play and learning* (pp. 195-218). New York: Gardner.

31 Smilansky, S. (1968). *The effects of sociodramatic play on disadvantaged preschool children.* New York: John Wiley.

32 Smith, P. K., & Whitney, S. (1987). "Play and associative fluency: Experimenter effects may be responsible for previous positive findings." *Developmental Psychology, 23* (1), 49-53.

33 Sylva, K., Bruner, J.S., & Genova, P. (1976). "The role of play in problemsolving of children 3-5 years old." In J.S. Bruner, A. Jolly, and K. Sylva (editors), *Play — its role in development and evolution* (pp. 244-257). New York: Basic Books.

34 Vygotsky, L. S. (1978). *Mind in society: The development of higher psychological processes* (M. Cole, V. John-Steiner, S. Scribner, and E. Souberman, editors). Cambridge, MA: Harvard University Press.

35 Williamson, P. A., & Silvern, S. B. (1991). "Thematic-fantasy play and story comprehension." In J.F. Christie (editor), *Play and early literacy development* (pp. 69-90). Albany: State University of New York Press.

Doris Pronin Fromberg is Professor of Education and Director, Early Childhood Teacher Education at Hofstra University where she also served as Chairperson, Department of Curriculum and Teaching. She teaches graduate courses in early childhood curriculum and early literacy. She is past president of the National Association of Early Childhood Teacher Educators and is an advocate for high-quality early childhood teacher and administrator education. Her publications include: *The Full-Day Kindergarten: Planning and Practicing a Dynamic Themes Curriculum* (second edition), Teachers College Press, *The Encyclopedia of Early Childhood Education* co-edited with Leslie Williams (Garland) and *Play from Birth to Twelve and Beyond* co-edited with Doris Bergen (in press, 1998, Garland).

THE VALUE OF PLAY

Observing
Children's Play

by Margaret Cooney

Diane, an early childhood education teacher, wonders why some children in her inclusive pre-kindergarten classroom can enter ongoing plan and why others have such difficulty. She thinks the children who receive special education services have more problems with this than the other children. Diane hypothesizes to her director that if she could help all the children with their play entry skills, the social skills level of the entire group would improve. Diane further speculates that more advanced social skills would positively impact the children's cognitive, language, affective, and physical development (Oglietti, 1997).

In order for Diane to help the children in her classroom with their play entry skills, she will first have to spend some time observing their play. She needs to know where they are developmentally, what play entry strategies they are using, and which ones result in successful *bids*. Then she can reinforce the successful strategies and teach them directly or indirectly to the children in her classroom.

This entire process depends upon Diane's ability to collect useful observation records of the children at play. She will need guidance and support from her director to master observation and recording skills.

Observing and recording play benefits children

Communicating the value of observing and recording children's play in order to benefit the children themselves is an important contribution her director can make to Diane's plan. According to our profession, observation is the early childhood teacher's most effective means of assessment (NAEYC, 1988; NAEYC/NAECS, 1991). Teachers can use it in the following ways.

• **Informing the curriculum.** Using observation to inform the curriculum is a developmentally appropriate practice. It tells the

teacher where the children are developmentally, both as a group and as individuals. It builds teacher understandings about how the children themselves see their world. It provides the teacher with valuable information about the children's interest and becomes fuel for the emergent curriculum (Jones & Nimmo, 1994). Recalling the vignette describing Diane's goal, let's examine how she used observation to inform the curriculum.

Diane videotaped the children playing in order to make wise decisions about curricular activities to meet her social development goal. She viewed the videotapes and identified successful play entry behaviors. Diane discovered that the children who watched play before entering were more successful. She also observed that the children who were more persistent, that is, tried more than one time with more than one strategy, were most successful. Diane confessed her surprise that children responded more favorably to nonverbal strategies than the "use your words and ask if you can play" strategy typically recommended by teachers! Diane planned some puppetry curriculum activities for her circle time. She based these activities on what she learned about successful social skills during play. Diane also facilitated children's entry into play groups when they needed help (Oglietti, 1997).

As a result of observing, the teacher can make wise decisions about curriculum activities to effectively meet her goals. She learns how to facilitate the children's development during play and during the other daily activities.

• **Communicating with parents.** Using observations as a basis for talking with parents creates opportunities for both parents and teachers to share what the child can do at home and at school. As they take turns sharing stories based on their observations, a more realistic picture of the child is painted. Thus, the parent-teacher partnership, designed to benefit the child's growth and development, is born. The outcome solves an age-old problem of discrepancy between parent and teacher perspectives regarding what the child can and cannot do. When the competency is grounded in a specific context, it is better understood. Both informal and formal conferences between parents and teachers based upon observation benefit the child by providing uniformity in his life.

• **Identifying children with special needs.** Observation and recording techniques used routinely by the teacher can provide important and specific data to support the teacher's impression of a child's needs. Through observation of children at play, the experienced observer gains insights into all areas of child development. For example, Diane's videotaped observations allowed her to watch specific children at play to determine their skill at entering play groups. During this process, Diane noticed that two of the children consistently utilized two play entry strategies that were unsuccessful. They disrupted the ongoing play and seemed unaware of peer emotions. These observations provided important information to Diane about how to help the two children learn successful play entry strategies.

Because children's play tends to reveal their highest levels of development, observing them during play gives their teacher a more accurate view of their competence (Vygotsky, 1978). Teachers have reported surprise upon watching videotaped clips of children in their program identified with special needs who were successfully demonstrating skills from their Individual Education Plans (IEPs) during play (A. Sullivan, personal communication, August 10, 1997). For example, a male child with an identified delay in personal-social skill development demonstrated social skills while playing with a female play partner that were considered beyond his competence level by the team who diagnosed him. When given the freedom to play in a natural setting with a self chosen play partner, he performed "above his head."

Effective observation techniques are powerful tools available to early childhood teachers for purposes of curriculum planning, communicating with parents, and identifying children with special needs. The power of observation lies in the positive impact it can have on children.

How to observe and record

There are many strategies for recording children at play. For example, Diane chose to do a running record of children entering play twice a week at playtime using videotaped recordings. Another teacher may use anecdotal records as a form of recording his observations of children's object substitution during dramatic play. Before choosing the best observation and recording strategy, it is necessary to take the following steps:

■ **Choose a naturalistic, familiar, and informal setting.** One reason observation is so effective is that it allows children to be assessed during their natural play activities rather than in a contrived environment. The children are doing what they would normally be doing. Furthermore, they are being observed by a familiar adult, rather than an outside person without an established relationship. The teacher, therefore, is in an ideal position to get an accurate view of children's competence, needs, and interests.

■ **Define the purpose.** Diane's purpose in observing was to design a curriculum that would build upon children's social skills. There are other purposes for observing children at play. Perhaps the teacher wants to find out the children's interests in order to plan meaningful projects or units. It is important to have a purpose in mind, even though the observation records can be used in multiple ways. Having a focus helps the teacher know what to record and when to record.

■ **Plan the time.** Deciding upon the times to observe and record is the teacher's next task. What are the best times to observe in light of the purpose? When can the teacher have some time to observe without too many interruptions? Times during the day or week when the children are engaged in child initiated activities often work best. Perhaps there is a teacher's assistant or parent available at certain times during the week.

■ **Choose a strategy.** Observations require a recording strategy; simply relying on memory of observations is not effective. Additionally, there must be a clean separation of objective (the details of activity and context) and subjective data (observer's interpretations). Strategies can be divided into four main types (Bredekamp & Rosegrant, 1992). Each strategy has advantages and disadvantages and is utilized for its effectiveness in meeting the purpose of observing. The table above contains the strategies and their definitions.

Although these strategies are divided into four types, I believe they overlap one another when applied in the classroom setting. The teacher learns to trust herself to adapt the chosen strategy to meet her particular purposes. For example, I favor anecdotal records for several reasons. First, they yield specific information, yet are opened-ended and flexible. This open-ended attribute allows for unexpected findings to emerge. And second, anecdotal records are a realistic strategy for a busy and over-extended teacher.

Imagine that you are a teacher of a five year old group of children. You are collecting data on their interests in order to select a class project responsive to the children (Jones & Nimmo, 1994). After recording anecdotal records for two weeks, you and your aide both read over the data and find that the children as a group have an interest in cats, both domestic

Strategies for Observing and Recording Children at Play.

STRATEGIES	DEFINITIONS
Narratives — diary description, anecdotal record, running record, specimen description, log/journal	record of what is happening within the observation's focus
Time Sampling	record of what happens within a given period of time, using tallies or codes to monitor frequency of specific behaviors
Event Sampling	record of an event and what happens before and after, recorded while it is taking place
Modified Child Study — checklist, rating scale, shadow study	variety of techniques originally used by researchers and adapted by teachers for classroom use

and wild. You decide to launch a project that explores cat characteristics and habitats. The following anecdotal record is a sample:

Mark arrives at school about 8:00 am with his father. He runs up to Dan at the puzzle table and says, "Look, Dan! My dad brought me a tiger shirt from the San Diego Zoo." Dan replies, "So — I have a cheetah poster in my bedroom." (10/02/97)

Each anecdotal record is dated and contains the specific information surrounding the incident in which an interest is expressed or explored. Additional information beyond the children's interests, such as special friendships, is revealed through the anecdotal record approach.

Observing and recording play promotes the teacher-as-researcher role

Observations of children have the potential to contribute to the field by affirming or calling established practice into question. For example, Diane's play entry study affirmed the notion that play entry skills were linked to social competence. Her finding that the successful bids resulted from nonverbal observing and modeling strategies called into question the "ask if you can play" practice recommended in the literature.

Observing can be thought of as a form of data collection for the teacher who is engaging in research. Literally thousands of questions about young children's play remain unanswered. Just as Diane posed her question about play entry strategies, other teachers can pursue answers to their research questions by observing and recording children at play. With time and practice, Diane grew to see herself as a teacher researcher. In fact, she found a new question emerged from her play entry study. Now she wants to look at how children sustain play. The

teacher-as-researcher cycle involves asking the question, observing and recording to find the answer, reflecting on the findings, and then generating a new question to explore.

Vivian Paley, a kindergarten teacher in the Chicago Lab School for many years, is an excellent model for the teacher-as-researcher concept in preschool and kindergarten. She has written nine books about young children at play. Each book answers a different question but all are aimed at documenting the child's way of thinking or the child's perspective. Paley recognized that through careful observation of children, her curriculum could become more child centered. Her book, *You can't say you can't play* (1992) is the story of her approach to the phenomenon of peer rejection in play.

Teacher researchers have the potential to contribute to the body of knowledge about young children's play. They have access to the children who are playing in a naturalistic setting and who are constantly demonstrating the process of learning through play. All we need to do as teacher researchers is learn to ask the right questions and make a plan for observing and recording as a way to find the answers.

References and recommended resources

Bredekamp, S., & Copple, C. (editors). (1997). *Developmentally appropriate practice in early childhood programs.* Washington, DC: National Association for the Education of Young Children.

Bredekamp, S., & Rosegrant, T. (editors). (1992). *Reaching potentials: Appropriate curriculum and assessment for young children. Volume 1.* Washington, DC: National Association for the Education of Young Children.

Carini, P. F. (1979). *The art of seeing and the visibility of the person.* Grand Forks, ND: University of North Dakota.

Cohen, D. H., & Stern, V. (1975). *Observing and recording the behavior of young children.* New York: Teachers College.

Geneshi, C. (editor). (1992). *Ways of assessing children and curriculum.* New York: Teachers College.

Jones, E., & Nimmo, J. (1994). *Emergent curriculum.* Washington, DC: National Association for the Education of Young Children.

National Association for the Education of Young Children. (1988). "Position statement on standardized testing of young children 3 through 8 years of age." *Young Children,* 43(3), 42-47.

National Association for the Education of Young Children & the National Association of Early Childhood Specialists in State Departments of Education. (1991). "Guidelines for appropriate curriculum content and assessment in programs serving children ages 3 through 8." *Young Children,* 46(3), 21-38.

Oglietti, D. (1997). "Boys' play entry strategies in an inclusive preschool environment." Unpublished Masters Paper. Laramie, WY: University of Wyoming.

Paley, V. G. (1992). *You can't say you can't play.* Cambridge, MA: Harvard University.

Vygotsky, L. S. (1978). *Mind and society: The development of higher mental processes.* Cambridge: University Press.

Special thanks for helping to shape this Beginnings Workshop:
Lynn Cohen
Peggy Cooney
Doris Pronin Fromberg
Edgar Klugman
Betty Jones
Karen Miller
and Sandra Waite-Stupiansky

Margaret (Peggy) Cooney is a Professor in Elementary and Early Childhood Education in the College of Education at the University of Wyoming in Laramie, Wyoming. She teaches courses leading to state Early Childhood certification and mentors graduate students whose area of emphasis is Early Childhood Education. Peggy was the Director of the University of Wyoming Child Care Center for seven years. Prior to that, she was the teacher in the Laramie Cooperative Preschool.

THE VALUE OF PLAY

Documenting Play

by Lynn Cohen

The drama center has been transformed into a hospital. Gowns, masks, plastic gloves, bandages, Q-tips, stethoscope, flashlight, cradle, blanket, clipboards with paper, pencils, and a toy telephone are the props used by children as they engage in sociodramatic play.

Thomas says, "If you don't take care of me, I'm going to die."

Tory — Writes out a prescription on the clipboard.

Thomas — "Let's go fast, I'm going to die."

Tory — "I need to write everything."

Marissa and Tanika — Both girls are playing with the doctor's bag.

Tory — Finishes his report. Picks up a Q-tip to check Marissa for head lice. He looks in her eye.

Tory says, "You have an eye infection."

Tanika takes the role of Marissa's mother.

Tory — "Moms are not allowed in the office."

Marissa — "I want my mommy."

Tory examines Marissa and says, "Just one lump. Rubber bands are pulling on it. You need medicine."

Tory gives Marissa a shot.

This is a typical pretend play scene in my early childhood classroom. Children are learning about the world of hospitals through play. It is important to try to capitalize on this natural inclination by providing the time and materials needed for play.

In describing NAEYC's developmentally appropriate practices Bredekamp states: "The child's active participation in self-directed play with concrete, real-life experiences continues to be a key to motivated meaningful learning in kindergarten and the early grades" (Bredekamp, 1987, p. 4). Many parents, administrators, and teachers think because children are in school, they should be doing *school things.* Parents typically ask, "What did you do in school today?" Children in developmentally appropriate early childhood classrooms, where play is seen as a vehicle for developing literacy, math and social skills, would probably reply, "We played!" This may cause parents to feel anxious because they do not fully understand or value the role of play in the early childhood curriculum, although they value and promote play at home. We need to help parents and administrators understand the differences in play.

Play in child care programs

Here are some differences between children's play at home and early childhood programs that we can share with parents and administrators:

Group Size — Children learn to play in larger groups in child care programs. While some children may still engage in solitary or parallel play, their play takes place in the context of a larger group. A child at home couldn't organize a hospital episode or any early childhood circle game.

Materials and Equipment — Child care settings provide children with sand tables, water tables, woodworking tools, and easels. Clay and paint are sometimes considered too messy for home use. Many parents purchase commercial toys for their children. In child care programs, children can create, design, and invent their own materials.

Space — Indoor space is not limited to a bedroom, living room, or family room. Children in classroom settings have more space to engage in block play or sociodramatic play. Children can create a block structure and revisit it the following day! Children at home usually have limited outdoor space and equipment. Homes have swing sets and sand boxes, in comparison to play areas in child care centers equipped with outdoor apparatus for climbing and rings and bars for swinging. Children living in urban areas have limited opportunities to play outdoors, especially in inclement weather.

Time — In developmentally appropriate programs, play is an integral part of the day. Play is scheduled on a daily basis. At home, a parent is busy with household chores. Some families with busy schedules may skip play altogether.

Adult/Child Interaction — Teachers can facilitate, expand, and scaffold children's play in child care programs. Vygotsky (1978) believes that learning leads development. According to his theory, learning is most effective when it takes place within the children's zone of proximal development. The zone of proximal development is the area between a child's level of independent performance and assisted performance. For example, a child is playing with teddy bear counters. The teacher observes the child playing with the counters and assists by suggesting the child count, sort, and graph the bears by color or shape. Parents would probably not guide and discuss many playful discoveries with their children.

To eliminate misconceptions of play in schools, early childhood educators first need to help parents and administrators understand the differences between play at home and child care settings. Then we need to help parents and administrators recognize the way the play-oriented classroom supports learning. I write monthly newsletters and conduct workshops on topics such as early literacy or manipulative math. Many parents and/or grandparents can rearrange their schedules to volunteer an hour a week. I invite two parents or grandparents every day to participate in my room during play time for one hour each week.

Mechanisms to document play to parents are anecdotal descriptions of children's progress, photography, audiotapes, videotapes, and work samples. More recently, I am integrating Reggio Emilia's approach to documenting children's play and experiences through panels accompanied by explanatory notes, samples of children's work and transcripts of children's conversations.

Anecdotal notes

In my classroom I try to observe children every day. Carol Seefeldt believes the best way to assess an individual child is through direct observation. "Observing is probably the oldest, most frequently used and most rewarding method of assessing children, their growth, development, and learning." (Seefeldt, 1990, p. 313).

Children play in the block center every day for at least an hour during activity time. Dr. Drew Discovery Blocks as well as Caroline Pratt unit blocks are arranged on book shelves and in crates. I provide a wealth of block accessories to add stimulation, aesthetic beauty, and dramatic play content. Literature related to building is left in the block center as reference material for classroom architects and mathematicians.

For many children building and constructing is the most comfortable way to represent thinking. You observe children talking to each other about their structures and verbalizing block building plans. Acts of literacy are incorporated when signs for buildings or maps are created. There is evidence of mathematical thinking as children use the blocks to create pattern and explore whole-part relationships.

Here's an observation in the form of an anecdotal record of a child building with unit and discovery blocks:

*"Lawrence began to build a castle. He took several blocks and made an enclosure. He looked at the book, **Castles. A First Discovery Book** (Jeunesse, 1993). He said, "This doesn't look like a castle." I said, "ÒWhy don't you build up?" He started to stack blocks perpendicular, then vertical. He added block accessories and said, "The animals are the guards of the castle. I'm only going to make a sign." He drew a picture. "This is the castle with animals in it. The animals are the guards. Real monkeys, bears, rhinoceros, and a couple of whales."*

Lawrence used language arts skills as he researched literature and drew a picture (see Figure 1). There was evidence of mathematical and scientific reasoning and problem-solving as I watched him build his structure and use animal block accessories. Tori and Christine's knowledge of maps and zoos was observed when they built a petting zoo with blocks and labeled it with signs. (See Figures 2 and 3). Figure 3 is a map of the zoo for visitors to use as a guide.

Figure 1

Anecdotal records of children playing with blocks is an example of one learning center where you can record children's learning. You can use anecdotes in the dramatic play area, art area, manipulative areas, and

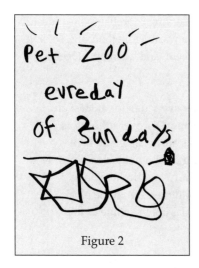

Figure 2

especially while the children are playing outdoors.

As you watch children play, write down what children do or say verbatim. Record the date, time, and setting. While watching, jot down enough information to get the basic story and most significant details. It is important in anecdotal records to keep information factual rather than subjective.

Photography

Keep a camera loaded with film to photograph your child's thinking and learning while playing. Photographs communicate to children, parents, and administrators the process of how knowledge is constructed. They also let children know you value their play by providing a

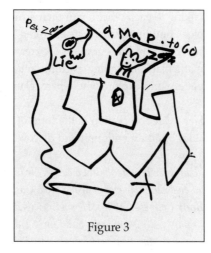

Figure 3

sense of permanence to their creativity. Photography provides opportunities for you and your children to look at and talk about play, long after blocks have been put back on the block shelves or sand toys put away in the sand box.

Audiotapes

Make audiotape recordings while children are playing. Taping your children's verbal communications will provide you with information about their language skills, as well as their development as cooperative players and problem solvers. It is useful to use audiotapes while taking anecdotal notes.

Videotapes

Videotaping play in the classroom and on the playground can be a passageway into learning about children's spontaneous play, their social interactions and development and physical changes. It is important that we ask children's permission before videotaping their play. Videotapes, as well as audiotapes, support our observations of children. It is impossible to see and record everything a child does and says while engaged in play! Technology assisted observations increase the accuracy of recording children's thinking and problem solving.

You can make video prints of those special playful moments if you use an 8mm video camera and have an audiovisual computer. Video prints can also be made from a Sony color video printer (CVP-M3). Tape field trips, story retellings, block structures, dramatic play, and outdoor play. Try videotaping the children a few times; and share the tapes at parent meetings, so that parents can observe their children's learning through play.

Work samples

Children's own work is the most authentic form of documentation of play and learning. Save all signs and labels children write and draw as they build structures or play in the drama center. Work samples can provide concrete information about development in literacy, creativity, problem-solving, and fine-motor skills. You can save the originals or make photocopies of children's writing and artwork. I often take photographs of a child using woodworking tools to make a math geoboard or sorting and classifying colored macaroni. It is important to date each work sample and create a portfolio or folder for each child.

Documentation panels

Many early childhood educators observe and record children's learning and development. Over the past six years interest in the preschool programs (for ages 3-6) of Reggio Emilia, Italy, has grown. Although early childhood educators have been practicing observation techniques for decades, we are just beginning to closely examine Reggio Emilia's use of extensive documentation. "Documentation in Reggio Emilia schools focuses on children's experiences, memories, thoughts, and ideas in the course of their work. It typically includes samples of a child's work at several different stages of completion, photographs showing work in progress, comments written by the teacher or other adults working with the children, transcriptions of children's discussions, and comments made by parents (Katz & Chard, 1996).

I hang presentation boards at children's eye level outside my room. On these boards the process and product of children's learning are shared with children, parents, colleagues, administrators, and visitors. Below are some essential elements to keep in mind when creating a documentation panel:

1. Focus on children's engagement in meaningful experiences (i.e., a project, a field trip, working with clay, playing with blocks).

2. Select photographs that relate to the experience being described.

3. Provide information related to the process as well as completed products.

4. Include samples of children's work.

5. Include a verbatim dialogue of children's discussions or responses by parents and/or teachers.

6. The aesthetic presentation of the panel is very important. Use a computer for text and enlarge photographs with a color copier. Mount text, photographs, and work samples on construction paper.

The challenge of adults today for the children of tomorrow is to allow the child to be a child, to do child-like things, and to value their play at home and in child care settings. Documentation of play provides us with an understanding of how children construct knowledge. As we watch and document children making discoveries with blocks, paints, and earthworms, we are supporting the future architect, artist, and scientist of tomorrow.

References

Bredekamp, S. (editor). (1987). *Developmentally Appropriate Practice In Early Childhood Programs Serving Children From Birth Through Age 8. (Expanded edition)* Washington, DC: National Association for The Education of Young Children.

Hendrick, J. (editor). (1997). *First Steps Toward Teaching The Reggio Way.* New Jersey: Prentice Hall.

Jeunesse, G., et. al. (1993). *Castles. A First Discovery Book.* New York: Scholastic, Inc.

Katz, L. G., & Chard, S. C. (April 1996). "The Contribution of Documentation to the Quality of Early Childhood Education": *Eric Digest.*

Seefeldt, C. (1990). "Assessing Young Children." In Carolyn Seefeldt (editor) *Continuing Issues In Early Childhood Education.* New York: Merrill/Macmillan.

Vygotsky, L. (1978). *The Mind In Society.* Cambridge, MA: Harvard University Press.

Lynn Cohen, Ph.D., is an assistant professor at Long Island University. She taught pre-school, kindergarten, and first grade for over 20 years. Her research interests are literacy and play.

Block Play

BLOCK PLAY

Block Building: Opportunities for Learning

by Harriet K. Cuffaro

Entering a second grade classroom, it is easy to determine what the children are learning. The schedule tells us when there will be math, reading, writer's workshop, science, social studies, and art. The charts around the room give evidence of and add detail to these categories; textbooks with their printed pages add further detail and content.

But how do we orient ourselves in relation to knowledge and learning when we enter a classroom filled with materials and active young children? What is revealed when we look at a child painting a bold design in vivid colors; another squeezing and rolling clay; a small group building a house with unit blocks; a trio preparing a snack with a teacher; a child absorbed in matching geometric shapes next to one drawing lines going in all directions to represent rain falling from the sky; or the busy group packing picture books, *food*, and the baby as they start their trip on the train they have made with hollow blocks?

Where are the categories that name knowledge areas, the textbooks that inform and guide what we see in this busy, active group? In early childhood education, our textbooks are the materials we offer children — the blocks, paint, crayons, paper, water, sand, clay, and manipulatives that fill our classrooms. Rather than books of printed pages with facts and information, our texts are more like outlines, openings to learning, entry points into the ordered knowledge of the adult world. In the hands of children, the materials we offer become tools with which they give form to and express their understanding of the complex world in which they live.

As they imaginatively experiment with materials — with the fluidity of paint and water, the unyieldingness and durability of wood, the soft malleability of clay — they bring their thoughts and feelings, and questions, to their activities. And in the process of experimenting and discovering, of giving form to and transforming their experiences in play, they author their own

texts, create meanings, and make sense of the often mysterious and complex world of which they are a part.

What learning opportunities are we offering children with the unit blocks designed by Caroline Pratt? As tools, what may children discover in using them? What texts may they author with blocks? While children's experience with blocks will be determined in large measure by the nature of the invitation we offer — the space allocated to blocks, the time offered in which to use them, the number and variety of blocks, the supplementary materials, and our interest and understanding — we can speak in general terms of the possibilities and opportunities for learning that blocks may offer young children.

Three year old Maria looks at the block shelves and takes a unit block in each hand. Carefully, she places each on its side with the ends meeting. Back to the shelf for two more units. As the line of blocks grows, Maria claps with delight. Next to her, Maya places one square block on top of another. Her wobbly tower grows until it topples over to Maya's puzzled surprise.

Four year old Maritza and Derick are working together. They begin by placing two double units on the floor and then two more across them. In a criss-cross pattern of double units, their structure grows quickly. At a certain point, Maritza's attention turns to adding cylinders in front of the tall building. Derick is absorbed in carefully adding unit blocks to each "floor" of the tall structure. Without conversation, each continues to add blocks to his and her structure and also decorations — colored one inch cubes, a piece of cloth, string, and a wooden cow on top of the tall structure.

In a group of fives, James, Grace, Michael, and Esperanza are discussing the hospital they are going to build. Michael has decided to make a garage for the ambulance. The others go to get blocks to make "the place where the doctor gives you a shot" and where "they fix your bones." On the way to the shelves, James adds, "I'll make the place where you get coffee and ice cream." Grace looks at him in confusion.

As they experiment with blocks, Maria and Maya have entered the area of *science* as they learn about physical laws and reality, about balance and the law of gravity (objects fall down). With time and the experience of many hours of handling blocks, they will learn, as Derick and Maritza have, how to make a steady building, how to balance weight equally, about three-dimensionality, and about self in space. And they will learn about the nature of wood: you can't bend it; it doesn't break; no matter what you construct, blocks always retain their original shape. In the three vignettes, we have examples of *social development* in play — solitary, parallel, and cooperative. Blocks accommodate the developmental level of the child and also the mood of the moment. For example, while capable of cooperative play, there are days when a child may wish to build alone. And it is in the block area that many and varied opportunities exist for *moral* thinking. Negotiation, compromise, cooperation, caring and consideration, and the balance of individual and group rights are not abstract concepts but concrete, lived experiences as children encounter and work to resolve the dilemmas that arise when space and materials are finite and must be shared. *Language* flourishes in this setting as children talk about their structures, explain the workings of their buildings, share information (and misinformation), and see the world from the perspective of another in conversation.

Block building poses further *problem solving* for children. There are architectural problems: How do you make the road turn here without a bump? Why does the bridge keep falling? While these problems are posed here in words, for the block builder they exist in the realm of the concrete. The problems are experienced through the feel of the bump and the sound of blocks falling. Initially, these problems are worked on through trial and error. Then, from an expanding background of experience, children arrive at an intuitive, wordless grasp of the problem that leads to action. It is from the long stretches of time spent in trial and error and action solving that children arrive at the point where they announce with conviction, "Well, if we add the triangle here, see, then the bridge will be more steady."

The harmonious relationship between and among blocks based on the size of the unit blocks makes this material a natural for learning about *math* which is about relationships. Blocks become tools that invite mathematical thinking. Patterns, geometric shapes, part-whole relationships, fractions, adding, dividing, subtracting are all experienced and practiced naturally in the process of building.

Going back to the three vignettes, we see Maria and Maya experimenting with and learning about the potential and limitations of wooden blocks. They are finding out both what they can do and also what does this (the block) do. In contrast, Derick and Maritza have mastered balance and steadiness; now they work intentionally to create forms that please them aesthetically. At this stage of block building, children often create breathtaking structures — structures they do not necessarily use in dramatic play. At this stage of building, it is the process of creating a structure that brings satisfaction to the child rather than a focus on representation.

It is in the block building and dramatic play of James, Grace, Michael, and Esperanza that *symbolization* and *representation* appear. From their shared information and what some may have experienced, the children bring what they know and what they feel about hospitals to their building and dramatic play. In Grace's concept of hospital, there is no "coffee and ice cream" as there is for James, who has been in a hospital's cafeteria. For the children, their task is to translate ideas, images, and feelings into visible forms. Blocks are the tools with which the children tell us the meanings they have created and the understandings they have achieved. As we observe their play, we find direction for our planning in *social studies*. What questions will expand their thinking? What trips should we take? Are supplementary materials needed? What books may add detail and information?

In symbolically recreating their world through their block building and dramatic play, children are also strengthening the skills and abilities needed for accepting and using the social symbol systems of language and mathematics. And, in such play, they often move even closer to actual words and numbers as they create signs for their buildings with their invented spelling, such as "Kasle," "Spas Stashn-2." The learning opportunities available in block building, and the dramatic play accompanying it, are many and varied. What has been presented is a beginning to which each of us may add from our observations of children. What has been said of learning opportunities extends to the adults who work with children. In observing and supporting their play, we are offered openings into the children's worlds, opportunities to see the meanings they have created, the questions with which they are struggling, and the stories they are boldly and imaginatively authoring about the world and their place in it.

Harriet K. Cuffaro is a member of the graduate faculty at Bank Street College where she teaches courses in curriculum and the foundations area. Her publications and research reflect her interests in young children's play and block building, the history of early education, and issues of equity.

Block Play: Experiences in Cooperative Learning and Living

by Sally Cartwright

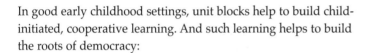

In good early childhood settings, unit blocks help to build child-initiated, cooperative learning. And such learning helps to build the roots of democracy:

*Five four year olds in our nursery classroom are building in the unit block area. As teacher, I sit nearby watching, taking notes. My interest supports the children. Our little school is in a fishing village, and many of the fathers turn to the sea for their livelihood. Travis and Noah have outlined a harbor with blocks. Todd wants to connect his public works garage to Sam's store across the harbor by road. After considerable discussion with the other children, he builds an elevated causeway across the shallow end of the harbor. Emily insists that Todd build the road to the main door **and** the emergency entrance of her hospital.*

Todd is reluctant, but others say how important both entries are. Sam gets more blocks for Todd. Travis builds a wharf on the harbor near Noah's lobster boat and tells him, "You sell your lobsters to me. I'll take 'em in my truck to the store."

"And bring some to the hospital," chimes in Emily. "We want lobsters for lunch." Travis makes a lobster car *(a salt-water storage float) with its shed and weighing scales (a square block and imagination). Noah weighs and dumps his catch (1" cubes) into the lobster car. Meanwhile, Todd buys some string at Sam's store. "Pretend it's telephone wire." Sam and Todd run this* wire *between their buildings. Todd calls over to Travis, "Want a phone at your wharf?" "Yup," replies Travis. Emily says, "The hospital's got to have a phone, too, don't forget."*

The children are absorbed in their building and play. As they learn important social skills and values, they taste democracy at their level through firsthand experience. When children learn to work together and help each other, they identify with group success. Conversely, the group depends on each member's constructive involvement.

In shared block building and play, the children themselves, ages three and up, learn to pool their resources and thereby respect diversity. Their shared structures — buildings, roads, bridges, and boats in three-dimensional boldness for all to see — engage their hearts and boost their self-esteem. It is their deep involvement, self-esteem, and warm mutual respect which help the children resolve conflict without violence.

In a good setting, informed and caring guidance often means that we provide a reassuring adult presence without intervention. In a good setting, the children's daily practice builds individual responsibility toward effective group process.

What makes a good setting for group building and play? Given a simple, relaxed, consistent, and reliable child care or classroom environment, there are six significant, interrelated parameters in the block setting itself which help the children develop effective group learning:

1. An open floor area with firm, unpatterned carpet is best. Up to eight children playing at once need a minimum 10' x 12' space. Traffic unrelated to blocks should be routed around, not through, the block area.

2. A sufficient number of unit blocks (400 for up to eight builders) should be stored — visibly sorted by sizes — on low, open shelves adjacent to the building space.

3. Keep toys and accessories stored in view and accessible, but separate from the blocks. Toys should be few, simple, and in scale with the blocks. For example, adult dolls should be about 5" high. Plain, wooden, homemade toys, which intentionally leave much to the child's imagination, are best. Where elaborate metal or plastic toys are used, block

play often suffers. Five year olds and up can make some of their own accessories at a carpentry bench.

4. Children should take from the shelves only what they plan to use immediately. An adult may occasionally and quietly pile up any stray blocks to keep the area neat and open for more building. At a specified clean-up time, for which — in recognition of the children's play momentum — a ten minute warning is given, three and four year old children should always return all blocks to the shelves. Ideally, if space is available, the block schemes of five to eight year olds may be kept in place for days or weeks. Building and play then become far more elaborate and rewarding. Adult help during clean up is often needed, and an adult role model is particularly valuable at this time. In contrast, except when handing blocks to a beginner for gentle encouragement, adults should not help children build. If you help a child build, she will not have done the work herself and cannot be honestly praised nor can she develop self esteem with integrity.

5. Blocks (and children) must be treated with care. While freedom for constructive child initiative is important, there are times for undisputed adult authority. Say in effect to staff, "Convey your love to a young dissident, but gently disengage him from the blocks and say with full assurance in your heart, "I can't allow that." Except for special, controlled situations, there should be no crashing of buildings, no touching another's building without permission of the owner, no hoarding, swinging, throwing, or dropping. No stepping, sitting, lying, or rolling on unit blocks. Although signs may be attached to blocks with masking tape, the blocks themselves should never be marked in any way.

6. Finally, adults need to respect the children (and their limits), trust them, and approach them with honesty, humor, knowledge of child development, wise intuition, and unfailing love.

Field trips, reading aloud, and group discussion are essential, shared enrichment for effective group learning with blocks. But, through years of experimental work, we found that as long as content was close to the children's experience, predetermined information, i.e. selecting which facts we would like young children to know, is not important when compared to the *ways* they learn. When children work together, when they pursue information through firsthand experience, through their own action, when they are curious, excited, and deeply involved in finding and using information, this is child education at its best.

In my own experience with children, their daily cooperative learning with blocks opened my eyes. This lively sense of caring purpose, this group intentionality proved a marvelous lift to learning. It drew the children to their work. It kept them going. Each morning, these small explorers shared stumbling, laughter, and plain hard work toward deep satisfaction in both individual and group achievement. Unlike the competitive atmosphere in many schools, our warmly cooperative setting invited unique, personal accomplishment toward group goals.

The process was intrinsic to the children's spontaneous building and play. Individual child constructions were soon linked together by roads, bridges, tunnels, pretend waterways, and, of course, by shared interests — Travis sold his lobsters; Emily bought and served them for lunch. By mid-morning, the youngsters had usually constructed, quite on their own, an interdependent community which they could *see*, *feel*, and *do*. This first half of the morning became a magic time of child endeavor, of group enthusiasm for learning which touched every child.

A remarkable outcome was the degree of sustained mutual concern and support that prevailed not only when construction went smoothly, but through frustration, fatigue, and disappointment. With open affection, the children helped each other. With caring respect, they settled their own disputes. Seldom did teachers need to intervene. Comradeship in learning made our classroom sunlit.

Note: In a follow-up study, we learned that most of these children won academic honors in the local public school. But what especially pleased me was their marked ability to meet new situations with poise and shared invention.

Sally Cartwright, a former teacher and preschool director with an MS from Bank Street College, has enjoyed 50 years of work with and for children. Her writing on blocks has been published here and abroad. Of the eight books for children by Cartwright, six have been published by Coward McCann, and two by Doubleday. As for her numerous articles on education, most have been published here and abroad by the National Association for the Education of Young Children. A number of Sally's articles were published over the years by Exchange Press.

BLOCK PLAY

Block Play is for ALL Children

by Kay (Stritzel) Rencken

The block center can be the most exciting place in the early childhood classroom. A center that is attractive and well stocked with unit blocks is an invitation to learning that will last a child a lifetime. Why is it, then, that in many classrooms it is only a select group of boys and the occasional girl who are taking advantage of these blocks? In room after room, it is primarily boys that are building with the blocks. In these same rooms, the girls are busy in the housekeeping center. Much learning is taking place in both of these centers. The learning that can take place in the block center is learning that should be available to all of the children — not just a small group that is usually boys.

When looking in your classroom, do you see the girls playing in the housekeeping center, the reading center, the art center, and the manipulative and/or math center? And do you also see the boys playing in the block center, at the computer, and the manipulatives? Probably your first response is "Well, a few of my girls play with the unit blocks sometimes." A quick way to check this out is to keep a checklist of who is in the block area for a week or two.

After you have compiled this evidence, you are faced with the question of "What do I do now?" There are some strategies to change where the girls and boys are playing, and to encourage all children to use the unit blocks. In some classrooms, a group of children will claim an area as their "territory" and other children (boys and girls) are excluded.

The first item of business is to review your feelings about unit blocks and your knowledge about them. Next, you need to look at where you spend your time during the period of the day when blocks are an open center. Are you available to the children in the blocks? Do you comment and talk to the children about their block play and building?

Blocks are not like painting and other art forms since you cannot display them on the walls of the room. They are mostly transient constructions. But there are ways to "save" them:

■ Leave the constructions up for a day or so.
■ Label the constructions.
■ Take photographs to display in block books.
■ Take dictation or have children write stories about their work.
■ Make sketches of the buildings (by children or adults).

Start a collection of pictures of buildings that can be displayed near the block center. These can come from art prints that have buildings as a part of the scene or pictures cut from magazines and newspapers. By displaying these pictures, some children who are unsure of what they should build will have some specific ideas. Taking walking trips around the school also provides some ideas for structures. Your presence in the center is also an important factor in letting the children know that you value what is going on. You can be there as an observer or as a player. Most of all, you can talk to the children about their work. You convey your interest using convergent and divergent questions about what blocks they are using, the time spent, feelings and thoughts about the building, who they are building with, the number of different blocks being used, what they are building, balance, symmetry, and pattern. It is also an opportunity to encourage the child to take another step in learning (Vygotsky's zone of proximal development).

Now that you are in the block center more often, you have probably observed that there seems to be a difference in the way the boys and girls play with the blocks. The boys tend to build and build and build; usually they are building elaborate and tall structures. Boys seem to build skyscrapers no matter what part of the country they live in. Girls often build much less complicated and smaller structures that they then use to play out a scene such as house, farm, etc. The boys tend to love to tear down these structures and the girls are often more willing to help in the picking up.

Building with blocks utilizes skills from all the cognitive domains like math (number and pattern), science (balance and gravity), social studies (copying architectural monuments), art (form and design), and physical (large and small muscle utilization). Playing with blocks is mainly a social event with roles being played out with blocks as the medium. Both building and playing are important skills in the block center, and the teacher's job is to encourage each child to utilize both aspects.

The classroom can be arranged so that the housekeeping center is outside during the first few months of school and the block center encompasses that space indoors. This puts the house-keeping center near the very active play outside and it becomes a part of it. When the children are inside, the girls often join the action in the block center and play there.

If you have boys and girls playing together in the block center, they will be learning from each other. But even at this young age, boys and girls are beginning to segregate themselves based on their sex.

They often have a view of what a boy/girl is based upon, where a child plays, who a child plays with, and what a child wears. They have observed during their previous years in group care that the boys play in blocks and therefore it must be a "boy place." In some classrooms, a planning board is used to help the children decide where they are going to play that day. With slightly older children, they can be heterogeneously grouped into committees so that during committee time or center time the group is working in the block center either with the teacher or independently. When the teacher does this, he is saying that the block center is an important learning place — like the computer, math, and reading center. The teacher can encourage the children to work together, talk with them about their building, guide their play, and observe their use of the blocks in play or building. Girls often relish the opportunity to become skilled block builders. They are using numbers and math concepts in a very real way. They are eager to expand their storytelling abilities to include what they are building with blocks. Boys enjoy dramatic play with the blocks in a way that is different from their play in the housekeeping center. There can be a time for talking and sharing about what was built and comparisons to buildings that had been built previously in the block center.

Most of all, it gives boys and girls a chance to work together on a real project, to share in the planning, building, and evaluation of the structure and possibly plan future structures together.

Early childhood educators often lament that boys and girls don't play together often enough. Building and playing with unit blocks provides opportunities for them to play and learn together from this most valuable tool — the unit blocks.

Kay (Stritzel) Rencken, MA, is a retired kindergarten teacher and Pacific Oaks Adjunct Faculty who now volunteers in early childhood settings, works as a consultant, and is active in SAzAEYC.

BLOCK PLAY

Enriching the Possbilities of Block Play

by Stuart Reifel

Children enjoy playing with all sorts of blocks, including large blocks for building forts and castles, plastic snap-blocks for making robots, animals, airplanes, or cars, table-top blocks for creating patterns or settings for small dolls, and all other types of construction materials. Unit blocks, made from wood in standard, mathematically related shapes and sizes, are a valuable part of many early childhood settings. The fun that children have with all these types of blocks is enhanced by the fact that blocks provide children with opportunities to develop and learn. As children play with blocks, they develop under-standings about geometry and physical space, they acquire concepts, they learn to create and represent meanings, and they find ways to work together to solve disagreements (Hirsch, 1984). A great deal can be done by teachers to help learning happen with different types of blocks.

We know from years of research and teaching that children develop as they play with blocks. All children begin by exploring the qualities of blocks, including size, shape, weight, texture, and color. When a teacher talks about those qualities while children are exploring, it gives children valuable language that is linked to their experiences. Teacher talk also lets children know that what they are doing with blocks is valued. As children begin to put blocks together, they begin to learn about length, height, volume, physical space, and the power they can feel as they control it. By creating shapes with blocks, we begin to see how we give shape to our lives (Erikson, 1963; Piaget, 1962).

By the time children are two or three years old, their block play is nearly always about something. Children may create a shape, but they then decide that what they have made is a spaceship or a house for their dolls. Piaget tells us that block play is a kind of symbolic representation. Children create and playa with meanings that are important to them, whether the meanings relate to home and babies, farms and animals, spaceships and monsters, or Power Rangers. Much block play shows us what people are thinking about. It is as children represent while they play with blocks that we can enrich their experiences.

Setting up space and props

A neat, inviting arrangement of blocks in well organized storage cases will encourage play. An area of the room partitioned from other areas can create a comfortable space for exploring with blocks. Partitions can also direct traffic around block play, so constructions will not be bumped by children in transition from one activity to another. By using movable shelves for storage, the play space can be changed from time to time to make block play a part of other play areas in the room. Block play areas should not be totally secluded; adults should be able to supervise and offer guidance for players, and other children (especially girls!) should be able to relate their play to what goes on with blocks.

Because children explore space as they build with unit blocks, they need space in which to build. Some teachers prefer a carpeted area for block play in their classrooms to reduce noise from falling blocks. Many carpets are too soft or have irregular nap, making construction impossible; a flat, even surface works best. Some teachers appreciate the joy that crashing blocks can provide for children and use no carpet at all. In either case, a space large enough for three to five children to build together is necessary; with moveable partitions, the space can be made larger should more children want to join.

Table-top blocks, plastic snap-blocks, and other smaller blocks also need to be stored in attractive containers that are well marked so that children know where to find them and how to return them to their places. As children show interest, smaller blocks in their storage containers might be brought into the unit block area to increase play opportunities. Plastic block cars or animals might contribute to unit block roadways or zoos. Just as small blocks can be brought into the unit block area, other dramatic play toys can be used there. Toy animals, cars, dolls, tea sets, airplanes, and other toys can be introduced to the block area, possibly after a story or a field trip that relates to those toys. Pictures, posted on the walls, related to stories or field trips, may promote block construction. Including props helps suggest what block play might be about, but children will always bring their own ideas to their play.

Integrating blocks with other types of play

We can see from our discussion above that play with manipulative, like plastic snap-blocks, can be brought into unit block play. In a similar way, all kinds of play can enrich block play, just as block play can enrich dramatic play, art, music, and language plan. By having dress-up clothes in or near the block area, you may suggest any number of construction play themes — fire station, bakery, grocery store, and airplane. Hats, jackets, and other dramatic play props can stimulate construction of appropriate settings for dramatic play. If your playhouse area is separated from the blocks by a moveable partition, the areas can be opened to each other; children can construct a living room, d en, or garage that is related to their play kitchen. Connecting the block area with housekeeping often increases participation by girls in block play and participation of boys in dress-up.

Informal art can also relate to block play. Children who cannot build a block house with windows may draw windows on paper and tape them onto their block houses. Trees, animals, characters, or vehicles that have been drawn with crayons or markers may be added to block play if children can find that they do not have the props they need to enact their play. Children might also create their own paper hats, painted capes, or other costumes for block play; they create their own props. Painting, drawing, and paper art can be brought to the blocks, as can hard-drying clay or dough sculpture. Children can make animals, food, or vehicles that they can add to block play.

Play related to language in many forms can be a part of block play (Garvey, 1990). Story books, videos, and television can suggest themes foir play with blocks, especially when related props are available. Read a fairy tale to the children, then put possible costumes, animals, or other props from the story into the block area; children will recreate the story, using dialogue from the story to the extent that they can remember it. Keep slips of paper and pencils near the blocks, and children will create labels to name their constructions. Include restaurant menus or telephone books with other block play toys, and children will build a pretend place to eat or a phone booth. Literacy related materials like menus, note pads, or real books can increase the level of complex language play (Christie, 1994; Reifel, in press). All of this is in addition to the normal play talk that children do as they plan, implement, and dramatize during block play.

Moving blocks out of the block corner

We can see that block play can relate to story time, field trips, art, and many other experiences we provide for children in our care. Just as we can bring any of those experiences to block play, we can bring block play out of the block corner to other areas in the playroom. If we are flexible, we can move a partition to open the block play area to a dress up area, allowing children to role play as they build. We can open the block area to a play kitchen, allowing children to use blocks for pretend food.

If children have an adequate preparation to build a town with roads, they might actually construct the town throughout the playroom, creating a complicated urban setting with different neighborhoods in different sections of the room. Children cannot explore their ideas of space and geography if we limit them to playing with blocks in one restricted part of the room (Mitchell, 1971). We do not need to be sure that they have a safe environment for construction and that the blocks are not used in a way that could damage them; block play near the sink could lead to water warping and ruined blocks.

Practical tips

A classroom needs to be arranged thoughtfully and flexibly if we want children to benefit from block play. You need ample space for a group of children to play together. The space should be clearly arranged so that children can find the blocks they need and return them when they should. There should be ample blocks to allow for interesting construction without conflict due to too few blocks. The building surface should be smooth and even to allow easy construction. You should be flexible about any space you set aside for block play; moving partitions and allowing construction outside of the designated block area will lead to interesting, interdisciplinary play.

Relate block play with other play experiences by providing props that allow block play to reflect field trips, books, and other non-play experiences. Phone books, simple art supplies, and any number of other materials can stimulate block play. Be flexible in allowing the block play area to grow larger as more children want to build, open to other play areas to stimulate dramatic play, or spread to other areas for representational play. Older children can sustain block constructions over days or weeks, so allow structures to remain from day to day if you can.

Children will create all sorts of fascinating block structures of their own. If you learn to observe what they are doing with each construction and with each other, you will be able to see how their thinking and skill grow. Look for the structural complexity of their play.

Are they making solitary, single structures, or are they building scenes with many parts? What parts are they including in their constructions? Are they putting all of their energy into building, or are they building in order to have a setting for playing roles? Are they repeating the same pattern of construction, so that additional props might help them think of new things to build? What kinds of language are they using as they play with blocks?

You can also see how your guidance may help them move to a more advanced way of thinking and playing. Observing block play helps us make sense of what children are doing, and it helps us to help them make sense.

Stuart Reifel is a former early childhood teacher and currently is professor and endowed fellow at the University of Texas at Austin. He is adviser for graduate studies in early childhood and studies children's play.

On the Floor with Kids!
Teachers as Block Play Partners

by Karen Stephens

Yes, I mean it! Hit the floor and become the type of teacher young children adore. A teacher who joins in and facilitates play, a guide, a coach, a cheerleader, a comrade in learning, a valued (and cherished) play partner. At least once in a while, slough off that aloof, objective observer demeanor. Jump from the block play sidelines and join in the excitement of creation! It's not undignified to play in earnest with children. And don't worry, you will still be "teaching," but it will be in a style that is better suited to how young children learn.

During involved and extended block play, learning takes place at a rampant rate. Most importantly, it is meaningful and enjoyable learning because the children construct their own problems and solutions as they develop block building strategies from personal thoughts, imaginations, and desires. All that learning means block play is serious business in early childhood programs; but who says that at the same time it can't be enthralling and intrinsically rewarding FUN — for children AND teachers?!

Woes of the well-meaning, but uninvolved teacher

When I observe some teachers at block play, I don't detect any true investment of their energy or intellect. They seem to lean primarily on one type of teaching strategy . . . drill-like question and answer. Their mind is not focused on the children's INTENTIONS, but on some prescribed "teacher-type questions." Oh sure, the teachers may be sitting on the floor with the children and it may LOOK like they are playing with children, but they often ask very simplistic, repetitive, and mundane questions: "Can you tell me the name of the shape you are using? How many blocks do you need for your road?" Boring! Talk about taking the fun and excitement out of block building! This style of teacher-child interaction actually communicates

disinterest in children's actual thoughts, goals, and plans. These teachers are not intentionally trying to duplicate the "testing atmosphere" many of us were educated in, but unwittingly many do so. This teaching strategy is insulting to and disrespectful of young children's preferred method of learning — **engaging and intentional play**.

Another concern I have about pseudo-engaged teachers is how they try to encourage block play through manipulative reinforcement. We've all said it: "I like how Joey is building" or "Tanya is being a good builder today." (This is often made in an attempt to influence another child into behaving appropriately.) Regardless of the purpose of the comments, little true attention and thought is required of the teacher to make such ho-hum statements. These "one size fits all" praise bites do not encourage learning or build self-esteem (which I KNOW are teachers' hopes). These comments could be said to any child. Our comments will be developmentally appropriate ONLY when formulated in response to SPECIFIC children's ideas. Praise alone does not build self-esteem; achievement does. The best way to encourage learning and build children's self-esteem is for teachers to invest their **time** engaged WITH children throughout the **process** of block building! What better way to pay children a compliment than to show them their ideas are so motivating and intriguing that you will set aside some of your time to become part of their makebelieve world?

The art of being a block play partner

So how do you begin being a play partner? It's easy (once you get the hang of it, that is)! First, dress for comfort so you can sprawl out while stretching and reaching; good block builders do lots of this. Second, get on the floor in the block area. While it is good to objectively observe from time to time, it is not behavior that leads to being an engaged play partner.

Next, think **play**, think "**pretend as if.**" You have to have a positive attitude about the intrinsic value of block play! As a good play partner, you'll need to lose self-consciousness that may hinder your creativity and spontaneity. Take the luxury of playing with abandon; it's the same principle children use in dressup play! It encourages the development of complex and sophisticated symbolic thought in children. Once you are in the proper frame of mind, just start building by yourself in the block corner. I guarantee children will join you if you are intensely interested in your creation. Children are curious when observing purposeful concentration in others. Of course, feel free to outright ask children to play with you. It's a strategy they use all the time! During play, be sure not to be a **dictator** of ideas — think **facilitate and enhance**. Listen for cues children give you while they are building, especially if you are working on a cooperative project. By being attentive and astute, you can encourage children on to detailed learning that might not happen if you were not involved. Following is one of my favorite block play anecdotes to illustrate my point.

*Five children and I were **on the floor** in the block area. Jessica said she was building a farm. The rest of us just joined in, no formal invitation was needed. Permission to play was inferred when Jessica began assigning us roles. As Jessica built a house for the farm, the other children casually gave each other suggestions and directions: "We'll need a fence for the animals." (Derek started on the fence.) "Where can we keep the animals when it's really cold weather?" I asked. Dickie grabbed onto that idea with earnest intention and started on a barn, complete with a ramp "so it would be easier for the animals to walk into." Joanie suggested we have sheep on the farm so the farmers could make their own clothes from sheep's wool like Charlie did in the picture book **Charlie Needs a Cloak** (by Tomi dePaola, Simon & Schuster, 1973). So Joanie sorted the plastic farm animals and put the sheep in the fenced area Derek was building.*

I commented that I always wanted to have a pond near my house so I was going to build a pond for ducks. As I was building the pond, Staley asked how I was going to make it look like real water. I told her I hadn't thought of that yet. With an enthusiastic sparkle in her eye, she said, "Let's use a pie tin from the art area!" "What a creative problem solver you are," said I. As we continued building, Jessica became bored with the farm idea, "Let's make this a castle instead and this can all be the manor" (her word, I swear!). So, by popular vote, the endeavor turned into a castle and manor. Jessica became interested in my pond. "Hey, let's build thrones by the pond so the king and queen can watch swans in the pond!" I agreed swans sounded more elegant than ducks, and said I was sure the king and queen would consider the thrones a lovely addition.

*And the play went on and on. Even a smoke house was built so the royalty could have ham in the winter. (These children were **not** vegetarians!) We took a block building break for morning snack, being sure to post a sign by our manor stating it was a work in progress and needed to be saved for us. After snack, we returned to our effort.* So there you have one of my fondest teaching memories. My only regret was that I did not take a picture of what ended up being a vast and royal estate. Luckily, the completed image remains vivid in my not-yet-senile mind. And, besides, it was the **PROCESS** of block building rather than the **PRODUCT** of block building that really counted in the children's development, right? (But gosh, I **still** really wish I had gotten a photo of the final creation!)

What principles can we deduce from the above block play episode? One, teachers should trust children's instincts enough to go with the flow of their thinking and intentions. Empower children so **they** can be captains of their own learning. Children's imagination should direct the creation. I did not dictate or direct. I did not ask about number, shape, or size, although I'm sure children were learning those concepts through "osmosis" as they played with the blocks and accessories. I guided children's thinking and planning by asking strategic, relevant questions such as "Where will the farm animals keep warm in cold weather?" Throughout the activity, I coached, I encouraged, I enthused, I admired, I played along with the fantasy. How do I know if I was a true partner in play? Because I had as much fun as the children did!

In the above block play episode, children were not passive, empty vessels waiting to be "filled" with facts, but were creating their own knowledge through concrete experiences with materials and peers. Just a few of the things THE CHILDREN learned through this play experience included:

■ to make logical connections (farm animals need fences and barns);

■ to make associations (if Charlie could use sheep's wool to make a cloak in literature, we could do the same in block play);

■ to take a different perspective for problem solving (farm animals need a ramp to get into a barn more easily);

■ to be flexible, creative, and spontaneous (if the farm is getting boring, change it to a castle);

■ to work cooperatively (division of labor is a real time saver);

■ to capitalize on each other's work (my pond was better because Staley thought of the pie tin and Jessica thought of swans and a throne); and

■ to enjoy the process of learning (of course, THEY thought it was just having fun).

Making it happen

You don't have to be a play partner every minute of the day — or even every day of the week. Plan ways to free up some of your time AT LEAST TWICE A WEEK to let you be a true play partner. Teachers who offer children opportunities to use numerous learning centers find it easier to "float" from one area to another joining in play. Teacher play partners need not play for long periods.

Recruit volunteers so you can have an adult:child ratio that allows you to work with small groups of children while other adults interact with other groups. Suggestions: parents, foster grandparents, high school or college students, girl or boy scouts working toward a badge, etc.

Allow for block play outside! I find children are often more self-directed in outdoor play (perhaps because it is more geared to their interests???). If most of the children are actively engaged in climbing, swinging, sand play, and the like, you'll have time to do some small group block building.

Block building offers many opportunities to pay tribute to children's specific skills, abilities, and achievements. When you remark on children's endeavors, respond with specifics more frequently than with generalities: "That was clever to make both sides of your building match." "Wow, what a neat idea to balance the curved block on the column." If you are in a rush, a general acknowledgment of work is fine (as long as it doesn't distract a child by interrupting intense concentration.) A steady diet of general praise reminds me of a steady diet of bland hospital food — it doesn't make much of an impression and it doesn't generate much enthusiasm. Those of us who have, through education and experience, gained knowledge of how young children learn must take responsibility for educating others about developmentally appropriate practice. It is a fact of life that not all supervisors or administrators have learned about the educational benefits of play. It is a true luxury for those of us who have such supervisors.

Until you are that lucky, you'll have to accept the responsibility for proving and justifying the validity of your teaching practices. Give supervisors a copy of **Developmentally Appropriate Practice: Birth Through Age Eight** (Sue Bredekamp, NAEYC, 1987). Give your boss a copy of this article to explain why you are experimenting with being a play partner as a teaching strategy.

I hope you take some of these ideas to heart. Put into practice, they really will make a difference in the atmosphere of your classroom learning environment. When you become a true block play partner, you just might get one of children's highest compliments: "Gee, teacher, you're fun!"

Karen Stephens is director of Illinois State University Child Care Center and instructor in child development for ISU Family and Consumer Sciences Department. She writes "Parenting Exchange," a collection of articles for parents of young children available at www.ParentingExchange.com. She is author of two books, including the *The Child and Adult Care Professional*.

BLOCK PLAY

Resources on Block Play

Brown, J. F. (editor). (1978). *Curriculum Planning for Young Children*. Washington, DC: NAEYC.

Burkhart, D. H. (1993). "Building Blocks, Building Skills." *Pre-K Today*. New York: Scholastic, Volume 7, Number 7.

Cartwright, S. (September 1994). "When We Really See the Child: Training Teachers to Observe Children." *Exchange*.

Cartwright, S. (July 1988). "Play Can Be the Building Blocks of Learning." *Young Children*.

Cartwright, S. (July 1987). "Group Endeavor Can Be Valuable Learning." *Young Children*.

Christie, J. F. (1994). "Literacy Play Interventions: A Review of Empirical Research." In S. Reifel (editor), **A**dvances in Early Education and Day Care: Topics in Early Literacy, Teacher Preparation, and International Perspectives on Early Care (Volume 6). Greenwich, CT: JAI Press.

Church, E. B., & Miller, K. (1990). *Learning through Play: Blocks*. New York: Scholastic.

Creative Associates. (1979). *Blocks: A Creative Curriculum for Early Childhood*. Creative Associates.

Cuffaro, H. K. (1991). "A View of Materials As the Texts of the Early Childhood Curriculum." In B. Spodek and O. N. Saracho (editors), *Issues in Early Childhood Curriculum. Yearbook in Early Childhood Education, Volume 2*. New York: Teachers College Press.

Cuffaro, H. K. (1995). *Experimenting with the World: John Dewey and the Early Childhood Classroom*. New York: Teachers College Press.

Erikson, E. H. (1963). *Childhood and Society* (Revised Edition). New York: W. W. Norton & Co.

Feeney, L. (1993). "Building Blocks, Skills, and Togetherness." *Pre-K Today*, Volume 7, Number 7.

Garvey, C. (1990). *Play* (Enlarged Edition). Cambridge, MA: Harvard University Press.

Hess, R. D., & Bear, R. M. (1969). *Early Education: Current Theory, Research, and Action*. Chicago: Aldine.

Hirsch, E. (editor). (1984). *The Block Book*. Washington, DC: NAEYC.

Kinsman, D. A., & Berk, L. (November 1979). "Joining the Block and Housekeeping Areas." *Young Children*.

Mitchell, L. S. (1971). *Young Geographers*. New York: Agathon Press.

Piaget, J. (1962). *Play, Dreams and Imitation in Childhood*. New York: W. W. Norton & Company.

Pratt, C. (1970). *I Learn from Children*. New York: Perennial Library, Harper and Row, Publishers.

Provenzo, E. F., & Brett, A. (1983). *The Complete Block Book*. Syracuse, NY: Syracuse University Press.

Reifel, S. (1983). "Take a Closer Look at Block Play." *Texas Child Care Quarterly*, 7 (1).

Reifel, S. (November 1984). "Block Construction: Children's Developmental Landmarks in Representation of Space." *Young Children*.

Reifel, S. (1995). "Play: Bases for Literacy." In B. F. Immroth and V. Ash-Geisler (editors), *Achieving School Readiness: Public Libraries and the First of the National Education Goals*. Chicago, IL: American Library Association.

Reifel, S., & Greenfield, P. M. (1982). "Structural Development in a Symbolic Medium: The Representational Use of Block Constructions." In G. Forman (editor), *Action and Thought: From Sensorimotor Schemes to Symbolic Operations*. New York: Academic Press.

Reifel, S., & Greenfield, P. M. (1983). "Part-Whole Relations: Some Structural Features of Children's Representational Block Play." *Child Care Quarterly*, 12 (1).

Reifel, S., & Yeatman, J. (1991). "Action, Talk, and Thought in the Block Corner: Developmental Trends." In B. Scales, M. Almy, A. Nicolopoulou, and S. Ervin-Tripp (editors), *Play and the Social Context of Development in Early Care and Education*. New York: Teachers College Press.

Rogers, D. L. (Spring 1987). "Fostering Social Development through Block Play." *Day Care and Early Education*.

Sawyers, J. K. (February 1989). "Constructive Play: Ideas in the Works." *Pre-K Today*.

Stephens, K. (1991). *Block Adventures: Build Creativity and Concepts through Block Play*. Bridgeport, CT: First Teacher Press.

Stritzel, E. K. (1989). *Blockbuilding and Gender*. Unpublished master's thesis. Pasadena, CA: Pacific Oaks College.

Make-Believe Play

Make-Believe Play — Why Bother?

by Dennie Palmer Wolf

Marc has an old towel pinned around his shoulders. He and his friend Rachel crouch near the sand pile where they are stirring mud and gravel with a stick.

Marc says, "Goosh it up. Way up. Now add more soup."

"Pretend this water is soup," he whispers to Rachel.

"These for the carrots and pepper and salt," Rachel trickles a handful of gravel into the goosh.

Three other children go by on trikes.

"Pretend they're robbers coming to take our soup."

"No, just kids."

"Robbers."

"I don't want robbers."

"Yes, robbers."

"NO!"

"Kid-robbers?"

"Okay."

It is easy to believe that when children play running and climbing games they practice basic physical skills. If Rachel and Marc were playing with containers and liquids at a water table, we might claim they were learning simple science. But overhearing them talk about soup and robbers when they are stirring sand near some other children prompts lots of adults to ask, "If they are only pretending, what can they be getting out of it?"

So what are they learning?

Since the turn of the century, parents, teachers, and researchers have recognized the emotional importance of pretending. By watching children, we have seen that make-believe offers children enjoyment, a vacation from real life issues, a chance to try out different feelings and roles. Without contradicting those old ideas, researchers are now suggesting that when children pretend they may be practicing an even wider range of basic skills.

Invention. As they play, Rachel and Marc invent new ways of seeing gravel and water. That kind of insight is important in everyday life; without it, no one would ever have come up with using a coat hanger to rescue keys locked inside a car door, substitutions in recipes, or ways to drive around traffic jams. In adults, that kind of flexibility in thinking is behind both common sense solutions to practical problems and even new ideas in science or technology.

Jeffrey Dansky, conducting both classroom and laboratory research, suggests that children who are good inventors in play are likely to be flexible thinkers in general. Possibly, then, sandboxes and playhouses may provide situations in which to encourage flexible thinking. In place of the standard boxes and cans, you might stock the shelves of the classroom store with a few blocks or objects made from wood scraps by children. If children are puzzled, challenge them to see what they can turn these novel items into.

Imagining "what if. . . ." Marc and Rachel have skipped out of the sandbox. For the moment, they are somewhere quite different — in some cave or witch's kitchen. When children leave the here and now, they are exploring the idea of "what if" things were not the way they are.

This ability to think — "What if things were different?" — is an important skill. Without it, none of us would be able to think (imagine) what it would be like in some other time, place, or in someone else's shoes.

As young as two, children begin to play "what if . . . ." Work by Jackie Sachs at the University of Connecticut and Christine Chaille at the University of Oregon has shown that children can grow increasingly skilled at pretending they are someone or somewhere else. This raises the question of what might be done to encourage these skills. A key strategy is to let children know you value their "what if . . . " play. For instance:

- Talk to or compliment children about an episode of make — believe play that you observed. Don't interrupt the play, but mention what you saw and liked over snack or while you are helping them get ready to go outside.

- As you pass by children who are making-believe, offer a comment or an object that extends their play. Passing by Marc and Rachel, you might say, "Hmmmm, I smell soup cooking." Or you might hand them a pinecone, pebble, or whatever and say something as simple as, "Here are some spices for your cooking."

Independence. The two children making soup have taken responsibility for structuring their time, choosing their materials, and making up the rules of their game. Rather than depending on a schedule or the already — fixed rules of a game, this pair manages to plan and choose for themselves. In order for children to take charge and practice their planning skills, they need uninterrupted play time (at least on occasion). This means allowing play to spin out, even if it conflicts with another activity. It also means protecting a good play session from intrusions. Play materials should not be ones for which there is hot competition. There should be sheltered areas where small groups of children can play uninterrupted. Researchers like A. F. Gramza have found that large crates or cardboard barrels provide just the kind of privacy that children enjoy when they are pretending.

Language development. Someday not too far off, Rachel and Marc will be faced with learning to read and write. Researchers at The Early Symbolization Project at the Harvard Graduate School of Education point out that in this kind of play children put sentences together in a way that is similar to the way that the sentences in books build on each other. For as long as they continue to make soup, Rachel and Marc are practicing two basic skills they will need in reading and writing-relating new ideas to a topic and telling events in order.

As an adult, you can help children sustain and organize their play episodes in the following ways:

- Make boxes which contain props for different kinds of episodes. A trip box might include hats, scarves, purses, keys, tickets, and a picture of a car or train to remind children they can incorporate trikes or wagons into their trip. A birthday box might contain bowls, spoons, candles, and boxes wrapped (or painted) to look like presents. Label these boxes with pictures which suggest an episode. Occasionally add new items to the boxes or change the boxes.

- If you have to interrupt the play for any reason (putting away items, helping another child to join in, etc.), try not to break into the play. If children are playing bakery and you have to replace some blocks nearby, you might say, "Just delivering the bread for today."

What if play turns "bad"?

Both Catherine Garvey of the University of Maine and Ned Mueller at Boston University point out that sharing, turn-taking, listening, and negotiation are all a part of pretend play among children. Group pretending is not always smooth — Rachel and Marc argue and they may even fight about what can happen. But because their play interests them, children will confront each other, argue, and politic to keep it going. Throughout this process, children work hard at understanding other people and the social situation.

It is not bad if children argue or even if the play falls apart. Arguments can lead to figuring out a solution (like kid-robbers). When trouble occurs, don't leap to intervene. Leave children the chance to think through the situation. Instead, keep your eyes and ears open for situations that repeatedly lead to trouble. When those situations arise, offer children strategies before trouble brews. If superhero play always leads to someone crying, you might tell Batman and Robin to try saving someone, rather than capturing people. Or you might see that the child who is often picked to be the victim is safely involved in another activity.

In fact, a number of educators, researchers, and clinicians point out that play isn't all wonderful. The stakes are high in play — children fight over who gets to be the Mother or the only Batman. Less popular children can be cruelly excluded — because they talk funny or their noses run. Children push and shove because they all want the biggest bicycle in order to turn it into the fastest car or rocketship. When they play Masters of the Universe, it's a boy's game, no girls allowed.

But precisely because children care so intensely about their make-believe, these activities provide a kind of theater for noticing problems and issues. The writings of Rosalind Gould, George Scarlett, Marilyn Segal, and Charles Wolfgang all suggest that classroom observations of play provide some of the clearest insights into individual children's skills and problems. Passive or isolated children hover around the edges of play, not brave or skilled enough to ask for a role. Aggressive children butt into episodes they were not a part of planning, mow down the scenes set up by other children, and end up more feared and likely to be left out than ever.

However, these same authors also point out that play provides one of the best situations for working on or healing problems. Scarlett suggests that teachers spend time as co-players with isolated or aggressive children. As a co-player, an adult establishes a trusting, intimate relationship in which she follows and supports the child's play ideas. In this one-to-one setting, the adult shows the child how capable she is of being an equal (rather than weaker or meaner) player. Segal points out that certain props, settings, and groups of children can also be used to make play a problem-solving medium. For example, substitute wagons for bicycles — the wagons insist on cooperative play. Or ask a socially skilled child to work with an isolated child in setting up the housekeeping corner in a new way.

Do adults belong in children's play?

If play is so valuable, should we make certain that all children pretend for a half-hour every day, just as we schedule reading time or large-scale physical activity? Probably not. Play is a powerful context for learning because children go to it spontaneously. Because they are interested and motivated, Rachel and Marc get around what might, under ordinary circumstances, be obstacles: the fact that they have no real soup or that they can't agree about whether robbers belong in the play. Also, play teaches precisely because it is unscheduled and full of surprises. Because Rachel and Marc were just pretending (not doing a group activity in pretending), they had the freedom to ignore or notice the children on trikes.

Finally, play is an excellent example of what might be called the natural exercise of skills. In play, there are no outside cues telling Marc and Rachel, "Now use your imagination — work on your social understanding . . . ." Instead, the children

recognize for themselves when to reach for and apply different skills. As they continue their soup and robbers play, Marc and Rachel move back and forth between stretching their imaginations and buckling down to solve some very real social problems.

Does this mean teachers should retire to the sidelines? Hardly. If we look again at Marc and Rachel, it is easy to see the enormous contribution that thoughtful adults can make to children's play.

One of the trike-riding children (Nina) gets off and comes over to Marc and Rachel, leans down, and starts stirring in the soup with a stick of her own. "Where'd you get this mud?"

Rachel says, "It's our soup."

"I wanna play with it," Nina complains.

"We made it, it's ours," says Marc.

Nina hits at the mud with her stick.

"Don't!" Rachel and Marc shout. Rachel pushes Nina away.

A teacher, who has been observing out of the corner of her eye, comes over.

"Nina, they are already making soup. Why don't you make the cake?"

Nina hangs back, kicking at the soup with the toe of her sneaker.

The teacher squats down and starts digging a hole. "Well, here's the oven."

She notices the other two trike-riders watching. "Why don't you park your bikes where other kids can have a turn?" She talks to one of them: "If you can find a jump rope, you could make a phone between the two kitchens." She turns to the second child, "Let's go find some good sticks so you can cook, too."

Dennie Palmer Wolf is a senior research associate at the Harvard Graduate School of Education. She has researched and written widely on children's symbolic development.

MAKE-BELIEVE PLAY

Fantasy and Exploration: Two Approaches to Playing

by Sharon Grollman

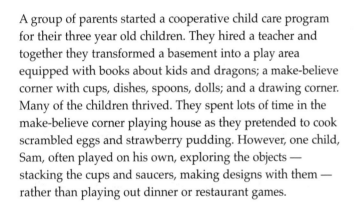

A group of parents started a cooperative child care program for their three year old children. They hired a teacher and together they transformed a basement into a play area equipped with books about kids and dragons; a make-believe corner with cups, dishes, spoons, dolls; and a drawing corner. Many of the children thrived. They spent lots of time in the make-believe corner playing house as they pretended to cook scrambled eggs and strawberry pudding. However, one child, Sam, often played on his own, exploring the objects — stacking the cups and saucers, making designs with them — rather than playing out dinner or restaurant games.

Both the teacher and Sam's mother were concerned. In the back of their minds, they wondered whether Sam wasn't as imaginative as the other children. Because they believed that more fanciful play was more sophisticated than just playing with toys, they worried that Sam was slow to develop.

However, if they had taken a closer look at Sam's play, they would have discovered that his play did not reflect a deficit in his personality or his development but revealed his particular imaginative style.

Sam's mother and teacher weren't wrong to believe that as children get older their play should become more fantastic. Much research on early play supports this belief. In tracing the development of make-believe play, for instance, many investigators have found that children progress from: (1) pretending with familiar objects — e.g., holding an empty cup and pretending to drink from it; to (2) transforming an object into something else — e.g., using a block as a cup and pretending to drink from it; to (3) pure fantasy — e.g., pretending to drink from an imaginary cup.

But that isn't all there is to the story:

Researchers at Project Zero, at the Harvard Graduate School of Education, have looked at the dramatic play of nine children. While our work confirmed that children do move more gradually toward make-believe, we also encountered two novel findings — (1) children show their own styles of play, and (2) these styles are likely to last over time.

Think about the different styles of play in the following pairs of observations:

Jenny, at the age of one, is given a small toy tea set and several small dolls. She uses the props to feed herself, her mother, and her dolls.

Annie, at one year and two months, is given the same tea set and dolls. While she uses the materials briefly to enact a feeding scene, most of her attention is devoted to stacking and unstacking the plates and spoons.

Jenny and Annie are also observed in the middle of their third year.

At three years and five months, Jenny is asked to play going on a boat trip.

Jenny: "Yeah, let's go in the boat. Oh, I see a wicked witch."

The experimenter and Jenny sit on the floor and pretend to look around.

Experimenter: "What else do you see?"

Jenny: "I see two plates. They fell down . . . and there's some doors and they are getting ready to saw us."

Experimenter: "Oh no."

Jenny: "We can go to Snow White's house."

The experimenter and Jenny walk across the floor.

Jenny: "Oh no, don't go in there." She approaches a small door in the hall and looks in. "Oh-oh, she's sick. We better fix her up." Jenny runs for her doctor kit, and a different scenario ensues.

At three years and eight months, Annie is also asked to play going on a boat trip. Along with Annie, the experimenter settles on a cloth spread out on the living room floor.

Experimenter: "What do you see?"

Annie: "I don't know. I want to get something else." Annie leaves, coming back with dolls and books from her room.

Experimenter: "Did you want to read books or just take them along?"

Annie: "Take them with us. I better get a suitcase." She does this. She unpacks small numerous toys from the suitcase. "I'll throw these in the water 'cuz all these are fishes." She packs the dolls and books back into the suitcase. She then surveys the arrangement. She points to the rug area around the cloth where she sits. "This is the water." Touching the cloth, she says, "This is the boat."

These two children are the same age, sex, and come from similar backgrounds. They have been offered similar directions, in similar settings, with the same adult as their partner in play. Nevertheless, each child has a different style of playing which shows up early and appears to last. Jenny uses words and gestures to create an imaginary world that unfolds independent of the immediate physical environment. Annie's play, on the other hand, focuses quite closely on the objects and arrangements in her surroundings. Her imagination works by exploring what is actually there.

Our observations suggest that some children, like Jenny, prefer pure fantasy while others, like Annie, tend to explore and build on the qualities and properties of objects around them. Jenny revealed her interest in fantasy as she created an imaginary world out of thin air — she talked about Snow White and falling plates even though no such things occurred. Annie's own exploratory style shows up when she makes careful use of actual objects to create her fish, boat, and water. While Annie and Jenny are both capable of fantasy and exploration, each child's play reveals her own particular style of imagination. Moreover, their individual styles last, at least throughout the preschool years.

It is important to recognize that both styles are imaginative. As one of the researchers pointed out, "Think about how most people would react to these two different ways of playing. They would probably say, 'Oh, Jenny is so imaginative. She really knows how to pretend.' But Annie is just as imaginative in a different way. Unlike Jenny, Annie can explore the objects around her and transform them into something else. Now I call that imaginative."

Our research suggests that these styles of make-believe are related to differences outside of the world of pretend. Children who tend to explore are alive to and interested in observable sides of experience such as quantity, shape, size, and color. As a result, they may focus on, and even excel in, the creation of designs and patterns. They may be shy or quiet in activities such as discussions, storytelling, or dramatic play. In contrast, children who tend to use pure fantasy seem to enjoy doll play, stories, and role taking in make-believe. They often shine in arguments and negotiations which occur in play. These individuals may also become bored and frustrated when asked to do highly organized tasks such as puzzles, counting, and classification.

What insights and ideas can our research offer to teachers and parents of young children? First of all, there is a need to look at ourselves, to discover where we are coming from, to understand what style we prefer and most value. For example, consider the physical set up of Sam's play group. The make-believe corner was well supplied, while there were few materials to encourage the manipulation and exploration of objects. Even the books were about fantastic happenings. The materials reflected the preferences or styles of the adults and not necessarily that of all the children.

In addition to looking at ourselves, we must recognize and accept our children's styles. For example, Sam's teacher continually encouraged him to pretend. Her efforts (which may have reflected her interests rather than Sam's) made him feel uncomfortable and resistant, which left them both frustrated. How then could she have stimulated his imagination?

She could have encouraged him by introducing a set of small objects such as blocks, tubes, beads, and boxes. Together, she and Sam might have used these objects to build a radio, gas pump, or space control box. Chances are Sam would have enjoyed gluing pieces together and attaching wires.

To get a feeling for an individual child's play, watch the child at several different times during a week. Ask these questions:

1. Where does the child spend most of the time?

2. What materials does the child use?

3. How does the child use these materials?

4. When imagining, does the child spend lots of time exploring the physical qualities of objects? Or does the child tend to create imaginary objects and places?

Now, as an exercise, choose two children from your classroom — one who is a fantasizer, the other, an explorer. Walk through the classroom, an area at a time, and try to see it through their eyes. Is the art area set up to encourage children to draw people and places? Do the pictures on the walls include designs as well as scenes and families? Can the blocks be used to build doll houses or to conduct balancing experiments? Does the play area contain a piece of machinery with levers, dials, and wires? When you read books aloud, you can ask not only "How does the dinosaur feel?" but also "What type of dinosaur is he?" "How much do you think he weighs?"

It is important to provide options for children who approach play in different ways. Children who are easily absorbed in the world of objects may prefer blocks, clay, puzzles, and books about nature and about how things work. Their imaginative play can be encouraged by having them transform a set of objects into something else. Other children may prefer playing make-believe, listening to fairy tales, and playing games which involve social exchange. Their imaginative play can be extended by asking them to create objects and places out of their imaginations. On field trips, children need not only see a puppet show, but they need to see an exhibit at the science museum as well. All kinds of imagination need to be stimulated, challenged, and understood.

Sharon Grollman worked as a research assistant at Harvard Graduate School of Education, Cambridge, Massachusetts, when this article was written. For more than 10 years, she was a senior research associate at Education Development Center, Inc. Working closely with researchers and practioners, she developed materials for early childhood professionals on such topics as early language and literacy development and inquiry-based science for children.

MAKE-BELIEVE PLAY

Infants Don't Pretend, Do They?

by Lorraine McCune

Learning to play with objects

Babies are like flowers in a number of ways — lovely to look at, requiring nourishment, often sweet smelling, and both, of course, show processes of growth. Caring for babies is hard work which has its special pleasures — one of which is watching them grow. Sometimes growth and learning seem so automatic in very young children that it is difficult to remember that children don't grow quite like flowers. Unlike flowers, babies learn by interacting with the world of objects and the world of other people.

Even though we know how quickly and how much infants learn, when observing four year olds in the house corner, it is difficult to believe that their elaborate play skills had roots in much earlier, simpler activities. But give-and-take rules and the ability to pretend grow out of babies' first social smiles. The sophisticated pouring and stirring has roots in the way that babies reach for and grab objects. In fact, psychologists can now point out a number of milestones that are gradually reached and passed as babies first learn to play and later to pretend.

Learning to play with objects

From the first hours of life, infants react to their social and non-social world, looking at faces, reacting to sounds nearby, molding their bodies to adults who cuddle them. In the early months, a baby experiences the world differently through each of the senses. Under six months, when someone places an object in a baby's hand, the infant does not bring it to the eyes so as to see it. When someone holds out an object for a baby to see, the infant doesn't reach out and touch it. By six or seven months, infants begin to take an active role in putting sensory and motor activities together, exploring both objects and people in a deliberate way. At this age, babies grab at objects they notice and bring them quickly to their mouths, moving their tongues and lips to investigate. Although parents and caregivers often worry about choking and germs, this kind of mouthing turns

out to be a genuine way of learning. Susan Rose and her colleagues at Albert Einstein College of Medicine have shown that babies who only mouthed — and never saw — objects can recognize those same objects by sight later on.

Between 6 and 12 months, infants pass a second milestone in their handling of objects. The work of Holly Ruff (also of Einstein) shows that during those months infants learn to examine objects intentionally. Between 9 and 12 months, you can observe the baby take an object, bring it to the mouth, then hold it out to look at it before popping it back in the mouth. As the senses and the brain continue to develop, children use even more comprehensive strategies for learning. They begin to turn objects over in front of their eyes. Later, they can hold an object still in one hand while exploring its surface with an extended index finger.

At first, children treat all objects — balls, blocks, dolls — in exactly the same way. Gradually, objects take on their own meanings. Between 9 and 12 months, babies indicate what they have learned about the differences in objects. For example, they bang blocks together or against a hard surface but stroke or pat pillows or plush animals. As I'll explain later, this is an important step toward learning to pretend.

Learning to play with people

Interactions with people are important for their own sake; just notice how a nine month old explores the face of a familiar person, poking and mouthing at the adult's nose, as if it were any other interesting object. Unlike objects, adults can provide special play opportunities for babies by offering them the chance to learn and elaborate on social games.

Jerome Bruner, of the New School for Social Research in New York City, has described some of the steps children take in learning to play social games, such as "peek-a-boo." Even in the early months, babies react to the disappearance of a face. By eight or nine months, infants react with wild laughter to a parent's disappearance and will soon begin to pull the cloth off their own or their grown-up partner's face in order to keep the game going.

The most advanced strategy very young children learn is how to initiate games. This skill doesn't usually take shape until late in the second year. But in the months between one and a half and two, children realize that they can throw the familiar "peek-a-boo" blanket toward their parent or nuzzle their own faces in it as a signal which means "Come on, let's play this game now."

Babies also develop games that combine people and objects. One familiar object game might be called "give and take." As many adults know, 15 month olds don't offer you objects to keep; you are supposed to return whatever it is, and then wait to take it back again. Adults may not realize it, but they are often play partners in another game, "drop and retrieve." As parents or teachers, we may sometimes wonder how a baby who used to cling to objects has suddenly turned clumsy, sending everything tumbling off the edge of the high chair tray. What may seem like frustrating clumsiness or teasing on the part of the baby is really an important learning strategy. As the object falls, the baby watches its path and may learn something about the way that spoons clatter and cloths flutter. At the same time, the baby also is taking turns with the adult (something that is as important in conversation or bridge, as in dropping games). The baby also begins to develop skill at controlling simple social situations. These skills are important for all future learning, but they have special relevance to learning how to pretend.

Learning to pretend

In order to pretend, a baby needs to grasp both object meanings and skills in social interaction. As soon as the child begins to notice and remember the differences between objects and their uses, object meanings begin to develop. At the very earliest stages in this kind of learning, children's knowledge is quite simple — hard objects are good for banging; soft things are good for rubbing and patting. As soon as a young child can trade turns back and forth with a partner, she has at least a simple understanding of social interactions.

In my own work, I have observed babies taking five steps which lead them eventually to being able to engage in pretend play. These five steps are usually completed between the ages of 9 and 24 months.

Level 1. Babies show that they know the meanings of objects. For example, a baby may touch a cup to her lips, run a comb through her hair, or bring a toy phone receiver to her ear. These gestures are usually brief and may seem almost accidental.

Level 2. Babies are aware of what they are doing. In fact, they are often amused by drinking from empty cups or pretending to sleep. When pretending to drink, a baby may make elaborate sound effects, throw his head way back, and offer a huge smile to a nearby adult. They want it to be clear: "This is pretend."

Level 3. Play is more complicated socially. Children bring other people into the play, directly or indirectly. They may groom an adult's hair or put a cup to a doll's mouth. On the other hand, children at this level also pretend to perform actions they learned from watching other people, usually grown-ups. For example, one 18 month old I observed used a small plastic toy (a screwdriver) to shave. All the while he made really appropriate facial grimaces.

Level 4. At this level, children begin to string different pretend acts together. A toddler might feed a doll, then put the doll to her shoulder to be burped. Or a near two year old could pour from an empty pot, then pretend to drink a cup of tea.

Level 5. Children begin to plan their play episodes. As a child collects the props for playing with dolls, he might say, "Play baby." Even children who don't yet talk show this kind of planning. For example, a child might hunt for a spoon and a bib before setting the doll down to be fed. At this same level, children begin to treat dolls as if they were alive or human. Rather than plopping a doll into a crib, children at Level 5 will make the doll walk to the bed.

All of the skills which show up at this last level of early pretending are later used by two and three year olds to construct play scenes with other people. This set of skills allows children to be involved in sequences of play acts with others, to share their plans, and to treat another player as an actor similar to themselves.

Facilitating pretend play

When thinking about helping infants to develop play abilities, the emphasis must remain on the concept of play. Children need to follow their own agenda for playing. Adults can observe the child's agenda, fit into it, and possibly extend or stretch it. But the adult's role is to be a responsive observer and a willing partner, even if a child's play involves nothing more than simple acts. If an empty cup is offered — accept it. And don't underestimate the importance of being an interested observer. Babies prefer to play in the presence of an accepting adult. Pretend play is more frequent when someone reacts and participates.

If possible, individual play between a baby and a consistent caregiver should be a part of the daily (or at least weekly) routine at home or in the child care center. I believe that a separate set of toys, especially chosen for their appropriateness to 8 to 24 month olds, should be reserved for these one-to-one sessions. The set must include items which are good for simple exploration as well as toys that will stimulate more elaborate pretending in children over two. Toys must be carefully chosen to be safe. This is a complex issue; a few hints follow. Toys should be too large to fit into a child's mouth. There should be no parts that might break off, are sharp, or might cause an injury if thrown or fallen upon. There should be no small spaces that could entrap a child's finger. Materials must be safe for mouthing. The set of toys must be large enough to engage children for as long as they can sustain interest. I have found that the following set works well for infants up to two and a half years:

small blanket (doll is wrapped inside), blocks, books (Baby's Things and Pat the Bunny), small brush, large comb, toy cup and saucer, baby doll with clothes (diaper, jacket, bonnet), Ginny doll and clothes, doll bottle with soft nipple, stuffed dog, toy jeep, Fisher-Price mail truck, sliding matchbox, mirror, toy mop, stuffed monkey, cloth napkin, white plastic necklace, round nesting cups, ping pong ball, popbeads snapped into necklace, toy purse, five-piece puzzle, scrub brush, pair of women's slippers, sponge, drum with a bell inside, jack-in-the-box, Grover and Oscar finger puppets, toy iron, play sunglasses with lenses removed, toy teapot, teaspoon, toy telephone, toy toolbox (hammer, screwdriver, wrench, saw, pliers), 12"truck, 2" Fisher-Price man

Usually I store all these items in a large plastic bucket which I set down in front of the child at the start of the session. For younger children, you could select a subset of these toys. To play with a 12 month old, a teacher could select some objects that promote exploration (like the ping pong ball and the jack-in-the-box), mixing these with some objects that the child might recognize and enjoy trying to use in simple pretending such as the spoon, the comb and brush, and the mirror. The baby doll and stuffed dog or monkey should always be included because these items are very central to later pretending. The point is to interest, not to overwhelm.

Conducting infant-adult play sessions

Frank Johnson and Jerry Dowling, formerly of the Milwaukee Child and Adolescent Treatment Center, developed an excellent approach to conducting infant-adult play sessions. They called these sessions Infant and Toddler-Centered Activity because of their emphasis on facilitating the child's own play ideas. Sessions can be as short as 10 to 15 minutes, or as long as half an hour. Each session is guided by five simple rules:

1. Prepare for the play session by child-proofing a room, or area of a room, so that there will be no need to prohibit the child from any activity.

2. Choose a set of toys (number and type of toys depend on the child's maturity) that will form the focus for the session.

3. Avoid having specific expectations for the child's performance. Instead, allow the child to take the lead in choice of toys and activities.

4. Sit on the floor near the child, watching and waiting for an invitation to join in the play. Try to become aware of what the child is trying to do, and facilitate these intentions. Never take over for the child; rather, remain in the role of a supportive partner.

5. Be aware that child-centered play sessions are special situations, not typical of routine interactions. If it becomes necessary to control the child or to take over play, end the session.

What is one of these sessions like? Here is a transcript of a mother playing with her 15 month old child using the bucket full of toys I just described. In this episode, we can see exactly what infant play is like and how an interested adult can support and extend that play:

Child: Takes the bottle out of the bucket and says, "Baby."

Mother: "You see the baby. Where's the baby?"

Child: Ignores this question and picks up the jack-in-the-box toy containing a plastic elephant. She shakes the box and gives it to her mother.

Mother: "Do you want me to open it?"

Child: Drops the bottle she has been holding all the while.

Mother: Opens the jack-in-the-box, making the elephant pop up. She holds it out to the child.

Child: "Elephant."

Mother: "Elephant."

Child: Drops the jack-in-the-box.

Mother: "Oops, watch it."

Child: Holds out the jack-in-the-box.

Mother: Puts her hand on the toy. "Do you want to push him in again?" Closes the box. "Cover him up, good-bye elephant."

Child: Loses interest and wanders away to the bucket of toys.

Mother: Discards the jack-in-the-box.

Child: Takes the mop and swishes it along the floor.

Mother: "Are you going to clean the floor for Mommy?"

Child: Discards the mop and takes up the puzzle. She touches the pig piece in the puzzle and says, "Oink."

Mother: Points to another piece, "What's this?"

Child: "Baby" (although the piece is not a baby).

Mother: Looks in the bucket. "You want the baby?"

Child: Dumps the puzzle. She places one of the pieces on top of the frame. "Oink."

Mother: "Oink, that's a piggy."

Child: Places the third and fourth pieces atop the puzzle and vocalizes. She wanders over to the bucket and pulls out the beads. "Baby."

Mother: Shows the child how to turn and fit the pieces into the puzzle. "See, they go like that. They fit in the holes."

Child: Takes out a plastic bottle filled with small toy foods. She shows it to her mother. "Bottle, bottle."

Mother: "That's a bottle. Shake it."

Child: Upends the bottle, but nothing comes out because the lid is closed. She hands it to her mother.

Mother: "Do you want me to open it?"

Child: Takes the bottle and discards it. She goes to bucket and gets the doll, which she undresses. She wraps it carefully in the blanket and then replaces in the bucket.

Mother: Observes the child.

Child: Gets a second doll out of the bucket. "Dolly." She gives it to her mother.

Mother: "Is she a nice dolly?" She smoothes the doll's hair.

Partner Skills in Play

If you think about older children, this play will seem disorganized, even boring, at first glance. Playing with infants means accepting the way that they wander around, discard toys, begin and then stop activities. It also means not reading too much into their failing to take what you offer or to pay attention to your neat trick. Basically, infant sessions are settings in which very young children learn to play in sustained or interesting ways.

Even though infant play is often brief and simple, cooperating adults need a number of skills in order to make good play partners. The first skill might be called observing. The mother has laid aside what might be thought of as her adult agenda. Instead, she concentrates on noticing what interests her daughter. Just as the play with the elephant is becoming complex (and perhaps increasingly interesting to the mother as an adult), the child wanders off to the bucket. But the mother follows the child's lead, turning her interest to the mop and then just as quickly to the puzzle. Similarly, the mother puts aside her ideas about what you should do with puzzles. Although she certainly models and describes how puzzles really work, she does not insist that the child fit pieces into holes.

Another quality of good adult-infant play is what researchers like Vygotsky and Bruner have called scaffolding. The mother provides a skeleton of possibilities to which the child responds. The result is more sophisticated behavior than the child could have performed all on her own. For example, the mother helps the child to understand that shaking and opening will help her get the contents out of the plastic bottle. If the mother had simply reached over and popped the lid off, her daughter would never have been sparked to try these possibilities for herself.

A third ingredient in adult play skills includes expansions. Researchers have long understood that parents teach children language by expanding on the words or short sentences their children produce. For instance, when a child says, "Juice," a father might answer, "You want juice, do you?" or "More juice coming right up." In this play session, the mother expands on her child's play with the doll. After the child has bedded down the doll, the mother expands on this routine by asking, "Is she a nice dolly?" and smoothing the doll's hair. As a play partner, this mother knows how to add onto what the child did, without taking over the play. If the mother had awakened the doll, dressed, and fed her, she would have stolen the play session from the child. The trick is to expand without overwhelming or upstaging.

There is one way in which the value of this kind of one-on-one play is immediately clear. Both child and adult experience a special sense of warmth and appreciation. But there may also be a second, longer term set of benefits. This type of play probably leads to broader knowledge of the physical and social world and greater enthusiasm for play and learning. This is difficult to prove, but how fully do we need to justify strategies which give full moments in the present and hold promise for the future?

Dr. Lorraine McCune is a developmental psychologist and the Chairperson of the Educational Psychology Department at the Rutgers University Graduate School of Education. She conducts research on child language and play and is a child development consultant. She is writing a book entitled *How Children Begin to Learn Language.*

Problems in Make-Believe: Real and Pretend

by W. George Scarlett

Not long ago an experienced director of a program for normal four and five year olds called me to ask my opinion on a problem she was having. Three boys were playing in a very disturbing way. The boys called themselves "robbers" and pretended to cut apart baby dolls. In the middle of some activity, one of the boys would cry out "The babies!" and all three would dash to the doll corner to begin hacking away with play knives and sticks at the dolls' arms and legs. The director and her teachers were puzzled. Were the boys just playing or were they practicing violence and cruelty? The answer isn't obvious or clear cut. Teachers and directors can, however, develop guidelines to judge the health or ill health of fantasy play. In so doing, they can increase their chances for making wise decisions over whether and how to intervene.

Is the fantasy mature?

In mature make-believe play, children create characters who are fanciful. These characters interact rather than going their separate ways. The actions are imag-inary, not ordinary; and the scenes are imaginative rather than straight out of real life. Mature fantasy moves forward with a feeling of suspense; immature fantasy remains fixed in predictable repetitions.

This question of maturity in make-believe is serious. Let me illustrate. Recently, I was asked to observe a three and one half year old — to check the child's speech problem. He did, indeed, have a speech problem. At lunch he hardly talked at all; and when he did, it was to indicate (by saying "Wahh" and by pointing) some food he wished to have. However, speech was only part of his problem.

After lunch I succeeded in getting him to join me in the doll corner where we played at drinking from empty cups. Other children joined us and developed our play into make-believe cooking, eating, and attending to doll babies' boo-boos. The child I was observing never got further than pretending to drink. When I ceased prompting, he began bringing me various cups and saucers to pile in a single location — play typical for toddlers rather than three and one half year olds. This child showed a very serious delay in ability to make-believe. This delay left him isolated, unable to communicate effectively, and far from progressing toward meeting future demands of a normal school.

Our three robber boys provide a different picture than this child who could not make-believe. By comparison, their fantasy seems mature enough for their young age. It has fanciful characters (robbers) that interact. Its actions (hacking away at babies) are anything but ordinary. And while we have little information about scenes, there is suspense in the unpredict-ability of when the robbers will strike again. It may be fantasy which is cruel or in bad taste but it is the bad taste of four to five year olds, not that of much younger children.

Is the fantasy shared?

A second way to evaluate the health or ill health of fantasy is to look at the degree to which fantasy is shared. By shared fantasy, I mean make-believe play which is adapted for another — as occurs in the give-and-take of cooperative dramatic play among pre-schoolers. Obviously, our three robbers are sharing their fantasy in dismembering babies; but what could possibly be of value in such gruesome sharing?

When children are willing and able to share fantasies, they open themselves up to pressures and support not found when fantasizing alone. These pressures and support prod them to develop and organize their make-believe. The demands of an audience or play partner push children beyond private day-dreams, repetitious make-believe, and violence that threatens to become real. Furthermore, partners in fantasy provide additional excitement and ideas to keep a child focused and thinking so that he does not become bored and move prematurely to the next activity. Like the audiences of playwrights and novelists, partners bring out the best in young children's imaginations.

Shared fantasy also requires rules — rules to govern which versions of characters are right and which moves violate the rules. Private fantasy need not follow rules: boys can be mothering, and girls can do as they please. But in public, mommies, super-heroes, and even robbers all conform to the group's rules which define their respective roles. This rule-governed nature of shared fantasy play forecasts the more sophisticated rules in games of older children.

Shared fantasy also is an important means for developing young friendships. For the past ten years, I have had a special interest in isolated preschoolers — those children who spend much time wandering around classrooms, watching others without interacting. When these children do play, they are as likely as others to ride tricycles, fix puzzles, build with blocks, or engage in the other types of play common to their age group — with one exception. They are much less likely to engage openly in make-believe play. The implication is clear. Make-believe play is especially valuable for fostering relations among preschoolers; its absence makes it difficult for children to relate.

The fact that the robber-boys are sharing their fantasy seems, then, to make it healthier than might have appeared at first glance. The demands and support of the group keep the boys developing the fantasy so that its characters and actions are mature enough. The well-developed quality of the sharing keeps the violence restricted to the dolls and unthreatening to the players — at least for the moment. The consistency of the robber roles means the boys are following rules rather than impulses. The obvious pleasure in the make-believe fosters friendship among the three.

Is there confusion about fantasy/reality?

This is a third question to ask when judging make-believe. In the excitement of performing their dissection, are the boys becoming so carried away with emotion that they lose sight of what is real or likely? It is not uncommon for very young children to become terrified in the middle of their own monster play. A boy I knew often played Count Dracula. He would bare his teeth, repeat that unforgettable phrase, "I'm going to suck your blood!," and then delight in the scared expressions on the faces of his peers. But then, quite suddenly, his own facial expression would match the others', and he would cry out in terror.

Possibly the robbers could scare themselves. Confusing fantasy and reality might take a different form. Thinking even for a

moment that they are actually Superman, The Hulk, or some other super-being, the children might perform some dangerous act, such as attempting to fly from an apartment window. Stories exist of such incidents; and while the incidents may be rare, who wishes to take chances? Might the little robbers find some real knives and hack away not at baby dolls but at themselves or others?

A third result of confusing fantasy and reality is that children avoid adapting and stay locked within their fantasy worlds long past the preschool years. They can have in fantasy what they are too scared or unwilling to try in reality. Pretending to be Mother or The Hulk is much quicker and easier than taking painful steps to learn skills such as reading, hitting a baseball, or avoiding lines in hopscotch. Playing at being mighty and cool saves children from feeling vulnerable when trying to make friends. Might our robbers use their fantasy to avoid having to cope with uncomfortable feelings in themselves — feelings about real dangers or about real-life situations (overhearing adults talk about a burglary or having a new baby at home)?

These, then, are the bad effects of confusing fantasy and reality. They give us reasons to intervene in a child's play when there are clear signs of confusion. But in the case of our three robbers, are the children confused? To answer this question, we need to be clear about the signs of confusion.

What are the signs of confusion?

The clearest signs come from children's reactions to their own play. When children react to make-believe in the same way as they would to real objects and situations, they are confused by play. Also, if children show no special pleasure, joking, or excitement in play, they may be confused about the boundary between real and pretend activity. If a child pushes a toy iron back and forth across a toy ironing board without doing anything else and with the serious expression that often accompanies real ironing, the very real way the toys are treated suggests the child is not distinguishing pretend and real. To the child, this may be ironing. This type of confusion without fear shows up when disturbed children care so much about the arrangement of plates on a table that they cry or hit if another child shifts them even in play.

The three robbers are not confused in this way. The doll babies are not actually dismembered. Instead, they are left whole to be used over and over again for pretend hacking. The hacking does not involve actual or even realistic replicas of knives, but rather invisible knives or sticks used as knives. The pretense is not intense; rather, it is playful.

There is a second way to judge confusion in play. Children older than three often mark their fantasy by saying things like "Let's pretend . . ." or "Pretend that. . . ." This marking is necessary for well-coordinated, shared fantasy. It clearly indicates that fantasy and reality are being distinguished, not confused. Can we say anything about the robbers' use of markers? We lack specific information as to whether they use markers, but chances are they do. It would be difficult for them to have continued so long to carry out this fantasy together without markers to indicate what the group should be pretending. Even if they do not use markers, it is hard to imagine them responding to the question "Are you really robbers?" with anything but a response such as "No, I just pretend." Furthermore, when I asked, the director said the boys did not insist on being called robbers, nor did they carry their fantasy roles beyond their group and the doll corner.

There is a third sign we might use to evaluate the boys' confusion. When aggressive play is both explicit and extreme — as it is here — the feelings expressed appear real and potent. The danger is that the fierceness or anger acted out on the babies will spill over into other activities. The worry is that the boys will rush out of the doll corner, stomping down block buildings, yelling, or hurting other children. This kind of confusion seems a real possibility with the robbers. However, it may not occur. Before assuming any spill-over, teachers should observe: Are the children unusually aggressive outside as well as within the fantasy play? If so, they may need help separating make-believe from other activities.

Should adults intervene?

Using the questions above, it would seem unnecessary to intervene in the case of the three robbers. Their fantasy is mature enough. It is shared, and there are no obvious signs of confusing fantasy and reality. Still, there is the possibility that the director's and teachers' worry is the best guide. (In fact, these adults did talk to the boys about their play.) After all, is it not better to be safe than sorry by taking control of the situation?

But intervention has risks. The benefits of make-believe play come, in part, from the freedom to wish and fear freely. Such mature and shared play is not a simple retreat from reality. It is a child's way of coping with reality. Within make-believe, skills develop, friends are made, and difficult feelings are expressed and tolerated. Any interface in such a valuable activity warrants caution. Too much control can cause play to wither and disappear. As adults, we may shiver at the violence of the baby-hacking. However, good make-believe contains its own natural controls. The boys themselves may spend their interest in hacking — better on dolls with play knives than on real children with sticks. As fantasy matures, the hacking may become surgery. Because play is shared and public, another child can come by and say, "That's mean." For as long as the boys are clear about playing, they will remind each other that the hacking cannot spill out of the housekeeping corner. For as long as these natural controls are working, my rule of thumb is stay out.

George Scarlett is assistant professor and deputy chair in the Eliot-Pearson Department of Child Development at Tufts University. He has written numerous articles on children's play, behavior management, and religious and spiritual development. His most recent books include a new text, *Children's Play* (Sage, 2005), and a new encyclopedia, *Encyclopedia of Religious and Spiritual Development* (Sage, 2006) and a new text, *Approaches to Classroom and Behavior Management* (Sage, 2007).

Play and Culture

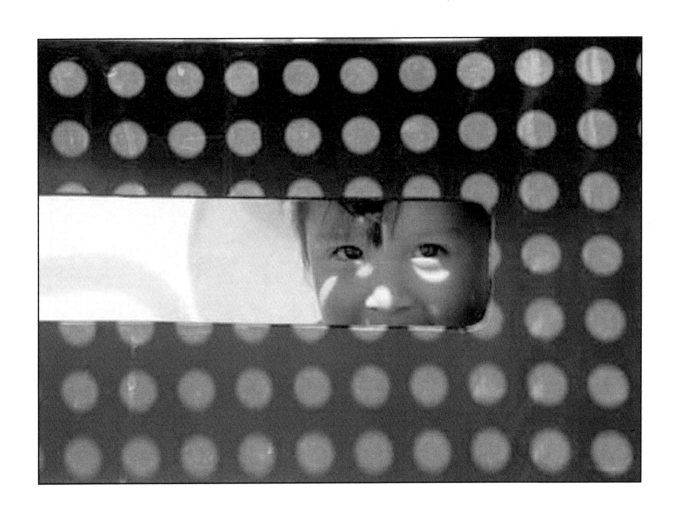

PLAY AND CULTURE

Play and Cultural Differences

by Sharon Cronin and Elizabeth Jones

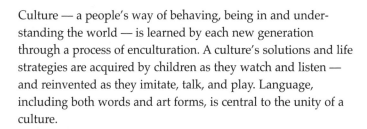

Culture — a people's way of behaving, being in and understanding the world — is learned by each new generation through a process of enculturation. A culture's solutions and life strategies are acquired by children as they watch and listen — and reinvented as they imitate, talk, and play. Language, including both words and art forms, is central to the unity of a culture.

In the first five years of life, children learn to talk their people's language and play their people's daily life scripts — homemaking and going places, talking to friends and buying and selling, making and fixing, singing and dancing, and storytelling and celebrating rituals. Children's imitative and playful grounding in their culture is the foundation for identity development and for trust in the world as a predictable and meaningful place.

For many children, this learning process is disrupted by racism and other biases that devalue their home culture, or by sustained discontinuous experiences that ignore it. A child in out-of-home care will be aware both of differences and of the unspoken values attached to these differences: Are my language, my hair and skin, my games — myself — welcome here? Am I expected to change in order to be acceptable? Child care can be an alienating experience — or an affirming one.

If no one in the child care program speaks the child's language, if none of the toys recreate home, if no familiar adult is present in a caregiving role, the young child is thrust into the confusing but all-too-common experience of *stranger care* — of long days in a setting which doesn't resemble home and whose people will have no lasting relationship with the child's family. In such a setting, it's hard to play and learn.

To some extent, stranger care is the experience of most children in professional child care settings in contemporary America. But children seek out reassuring resemblances even in encounters with strangers: Do you talk like my Daddy? Do you look like my Mama? Do you sing the songs my Grandma sings to me? What are we having for lunch?

Some community child care is almost like relative care — an extension of the family and its culture in a program where adults and children do share language, behaviors, and values. For children of the dominant culture, such settings may reassure them of the "rightness of whiteness" and the irrelevance of other folks' lives in *their* privileged scheme of things. For both adults and children in some communities of color, there is work to be done in recapturing partially lost traditions and making them directly available to the children — through artifacts and song-games and stories — for incorporation into their play.

Enculturation: Providing continuity of experience

The younger the child, the more crucial it is for healthy development that child care be a familiar place. How is this possible in settings where staff and children don't *match*? To provide continuity in children's experience — to reinforce identity development — it is important to provision for and support imitative and dramatic play reflecting the home experience. Here are four practical suggestions:

- Hire staff from the children's cultural/language backgrounds.
- Learn everything you can about children's home cultures.
- Provide representations from children's home cultures as regular aspects of the play environment and group times.
- Avoid isolating a child.

Hire staff from the children's cultural/ language backgrounds. Whatever any of us can learn about another's culture and language is only a small part of what is learned through early enculturation. The caregivers able to provide the clearest affirmation of a child's culture are those who grew up in it — who know from the heart its rhythms, its ways of being together, its assumptions, and its games, and who will share those regularly with children. *How did you play as a child?* is among the most powerful questions in alerting early childhood staff to the meaning of play for the children in their care. *How do we play?* is most readily answered for a child by the members of his own cultural group. And so a child care staff should reflect the cultures of the families enrolled.

Learn everything you can about children's home cultures. Develop a relationship with the community from which the children come, being sensitive to the things community members are and are not willing to share with an outsider. If invited, visit children's homes and neighborhoods. Learn phrases from their language. Read about their culture, listen to music, attend celebrations. Visit their grocery stores. Invite parents and grandparents to share something of their lives with the whole group of children, thus introducing more *scripts* for play.

Provide representations from children's home cultures. If children are to play their home-culture experiences, familiar props are needed. Do the baby dolls look like our babies? Can I carry the doll babies the way my mama carries my little brother? Can I fix a meal for my family and serve it in a familiar way? For some families from the Caribbean, a coffee strainer is a necessary piece of equipment in the kitchen; in a Vietnamese child's kitchen, a wok may be the first necessity for cooking. And who wants to serve breakfast cereal out of boxes with unfamiliar labels, when cereal boxes are among children's first reading experiences? Do the block accessories include animals and vehicles like those the children know? Do the dress-ups match what is worn by the men and women the child knows best? Do the tools match those used by workers in the child's community?

Avoid isolating a child. A child who is the only member of her language or cultural group in a child care setting has no one to share her familiar language and play scripts with, and thus has little choice but to assimilate. Assimilation is another possible outcome of the enculturation/acculturation sequence. It asks the individual to leave her home culture behind and try —typically with only partial success — to become a member of the majority group.

The burden of being a *token* is too great for a small child. If there are just a few children from a culture in a program, try to place them all in the same classroom, with at least one familiar staff member. If there is only one, recruit more.

Acculturation: Providing an introduction to the world of school

In the school years, children learn the expectations of the larger community. And so early childhood programs typically include preparation for school among their stated goals. All children growing up in societies not isolated from the larger world — and there are few isolated societies any more — must become acculturated to the unfamiliar. Going to school is always an acculturation process — but it is a very different experience for some children than for others.

There is the relief, for some five and six year olds, of discovering that school is a lot like home. The books and toys are familiar, used carefully, and put away *where they belong*. Behavioral expectations are familiar, and teachers even play the same kinds of games with words and numbers that their parents do. These children are perceived by teachers as smart and well behaved; their identity is confirmed.

In contrast, those children for whom very little is familiar and who don't speak standard English (or, perhaps, any English at all) are often perceived as deficient, troublesome, and in need of *fixing*. Their identity and competence, unperceived by adults, become at risk.

Child care can be thoughtfully developed as a bridge toward acculturation or it can simply introduce the anxiety of *going to school* at a younger age. In child care, children experience large groups, persons called teachers, and the things that schools think are important. Tasks that can be completed while sitting at a table reassure adults that education is happening and children are under control; children who attend to such tasks help teachers feel competent. But there are other messier and more active things to be learned in preschool, too — painting, block building, woodworking, digging. Many modern children don't have these experiences at home and may lack skills in carrying them out.

Children learn to play through interactions with more experienced players; in age-grouped child care, these are usually adults. If adults have forgotten how to make believe, or if the preschool has materials they have never played with themselves, then staff inservice training should include hands-on play sessions in which adults explore open-ended materials without children present. "Teacher as player" (Jones & Reynolds, 1994) is an important role for adults working with young children learning to become competent players; by modeling and suggesting, adults teach children how to play and learn.

Supporting bicultural competence

For many children and adults, cultural competence implies bicultural competence — the ability to *code switch*, to move with confidence between two or more languages and sets of behaviors, and to recognize which is appropriate at any given time. From very early childhood, children are capable of complex differentiations — between friend and stranger, between public and private behaviors — even between different languages. Biculturality, when successfully accomplished, creates greater flexibility and sophistication about the possible ways of being human. These are useful skills to cultivate in a diverse and changing world. (Chang, Muckelroy, & Pulido, 1996)

Homogeneous groups — composed of *people like us* — are easier to live and work in; no translations needed. Hiring staff from diverse backgrounds will increase misunderstanding and conflict. *Culturally appropriate* may not match others' understanding of *developmentally appropriate*. Language differences — and values differences — make every interaction a challenge. (Gonzalez-Mena, 1993) Teaching staff find themselves experiencing some of the same frustrations experienced by children and parents encountering the differences between home and child care. How can quality programs be created if staff can't communicate?

But this is the world we live in. We are not all alike. We have to learn to communicate, hard as it is — to problem solve, respectfully, with people different from ourselves. We have to learn to play together — with children, with each other — rather than to fight. We have to *use our words* — especially difficult when we speak different languages.

As early childhood professionals, we are committed to value each child, to create a small world in child care where every child's identity is valued and reinforced. We have to practice valuing each other, too. Children who miss that validation in early childhood — which is where it must happen, in the sequence of healthy development — are far too likely to grow up a danger to themselves and others, emotionally if not physically. Child care respectful of diversity and identity development, where children are able, through relationships and play, to learn who they are and who those other folks are, too, can make a difference in the creation of a healthier society.

References

Chang, H. N., Muckelroy, A., & Pulido, D. (1996). *Looking in, looking out: Redefining child care and early education in a diverse society.* San Francisco: California Tomorrow.

Gonzalez-Mena, J. (1993). *Multicultural issues in child care.* Mountain View, CA: Mayfield.

Jones, E., & Reynolds, G. (1994). *The play's the thing: Teachers' roles in children's play.* New York: Teachers College Press.

Editor's Note: Special thanks to Betty for her help in coordinating this Beginnings Workshop.

Elizabeth Jones is a faculty member in Human Development at Pacific Oaks College in Pasadena, California — and online, in the College's distance learning program. Her books on play are *Playing to Get Smart* (with Renatta Cooper), and *The Play's the Thing* and *Master Players* (with Gretchen Reynolds).

Sharon Cronin advises students in the bicultural specialization and the bilingual teaching endorsement and teaches classes in both the teacher education and human development programs at Pacific Oaks College Northwest in Seattle, Washington. She and Heather Palmer co-produced and wrote *Teaching Umoja*, a video and booklet on culturally relevant education.

PLAY AND CULTURE

Play in a Classroom of Iu-Mien Children

by Kathleen Evans

Most of the children in my kindergarten classroom are members of the Iu-Mien tribe, a people who came from the highland provinces of Sichuan in China and Laos. During the Indo-Chinese wars, the Iu-Mien soldiers fought first with the French and later for the United States armies. And so, after the wars, they had to leave their country. The United States government relocated them to American inner-city neighborhoods and provided them with welfare and low-income housing assistance. And the lives of the people have been transformed and disrupted in very profound ways.

In observing the children at play, the cultural differences are obvious. It is not unusual to see two or three boys collaborating with very little conflict to build one car out of Legos. It is rare to see a child playing alone. In fact, a Mien child's performance on the standard kindergarten assessment tool — draw a person — could alarm an American teacher interpreting it without understanding the cultural context. Until a Mien child has been at school for a while, any self-portrait will be a drawing of the child surrounded by others.

Unfortunately, many teachers appear to be unable to grasp a cultural context where sharing, taking turns, and cooperative effort are the norm and don't have to be taught at school. Teachers in the higher grades complain about how the Mien children chatter constantly, are unable to work independently, *cheat* by giving the answer to children who are having difficulty. These are just some of the ways the values of the tribe are undermined by the institution of school.

The challenge for me is to provide the children what I can of "the culture of power" (Delpit), while supporting them to retain what is beautiful and useful about their home culture. The greatest of these challenges centers on literacy. The Mien people have no written language. On the land, education involved teaching children the work of the tribe, the traditions, the stories

of the people, and spiritual beliefs. The teaching method used, from my observation of the ways the children approach new learning, must have been lots of watching and chatting among themselves about how the task was to be done and attempts at the task when one feels confident to try without failure.

The prevalent belief in our educational system is that good readers come from homes where they have been read to for a minimum of 1,000 hours before entering kindergarten, that literate children come from homes full of books and magazines and the mystery of print has been explained to them. This leaves very little hope that children from the Mien culture will succeed as readers and writers. Rather than give in to this deficit model, I have tried to support the literacy strengths I see embedded in the culture and to build on those. I see a group of children that have a rich oral tradition, the ability to memorize long and complicated stories. I see children whose involvement in art and music and with math materials indicates a complex understanding of pattern and the ability not only to recreate it but also to create it. I see a group of children who can work together well, so that a strong foundation to create a community of readers and writers already exists.

I value these competencies, and I try to teach in ways that reflect the way children learn at home. I try to create in the classroom the environment of a literate home, where children can talk and play in ways familiar to them, while introducing them to the skills of *the culture of power* as well. Through observation, chats with the children, group discussions in the classroom, my alliances with Mien adults, and my own reflection, I search for ways to include the children's home culture in my classroom without violating the sacred things that do not rightfully belong outside the boundaries of the home and the tribe.

We began the year with the familiar — with a walk to each child's house and a variety of storybooks and poems about houses. I observed the children's art and block play, where I saw how groups building isolated structures evolved into their connecting their structures with roads and walls and passages. Paintings of houses, which began as rectangles with triangular roofs and chimneys, evolved into more and more details as children looked at and thought more about different kinds of houses. And as they played, painted, and drew, their conversations included more and more words and concepts about houses than when we began.

The hospital is a dramatic play center that I include each year after the third month of school. Most of the children have had fairly significant experiences with hospitals, either their own experiences or those of a sibling. Our local children's hospital has developed a full service clinic to deal with the pediatric health problems in the Mien community. Most parents still use traditional forms of healing along with these services, so children have an array of issues to resolve about the hospital. Usually dolls are transported from the house to the hospital with a great deal of commotion, discussion, and excitement.

Each of the play activities served as a rich opportunity for children to use language, slipping fluidly between English and Mien as the play warranted. This talk is more important to the children's development of bilingualism than any other activity or lesson I could have provided.

As I watched and listened, I discovered children's recurring cultural themes and confusions. For example, from drawings, dictated stories, and chats, I found out how important fishing was to the families. In the water table, I included fishing poles, magnetic fish, rubber sea creatures, rocks, shells, and tin buckets. This became an engaging and important place to play. Unfortunately, it only had room for three children, and many more wanted to fish. So they invented fishing poles — the long deep sea kind — from construction toys. On the pillows which functioned as the bank, they fished, laughed, and joked for all of play time.

The way I set up and stocked the play house provided me with some interesting insights into the children's culture. Without thought, I included a high chair, although I have never seen a high chair in a Mien home. Before I knew it, the children, not the dolls, were sitting in the high chair. Before I thought to remove it, it was as broken as the wee bear's chair.

More successful accessories in the house were the Chinese dishes. Toward the middle of the year, a group of children had taken to carefully arranging the dishes, the flowers, and artificial fruit into a shrine, and kneeling to pray. They did this without self-consciousness in a most natural way. But the issue of making the sacred profane did come up for me, although I kept it to myself because the children were completely unaware that my teammate and I had noticed them.

The bookstore was another emergent idea. Each day in our class began with *reading on the rug*, a time when children may choose to look at a variety of books, use the flannel board stories, and listen to story tapes. Each day, a small group of children would take nearly all the picture books from the low shelf and arrange them on a round table. There would be a great deal of chattering and discussion in and out of Mien and English, with children leaving with several books and returning within a few minutes to get another stack. Observing during this time for *literacy behaviors*, I did not see the children as particularly *engaged in books or reading-like behaviors.* That is, not until I asked just what they were doing. "We're having a bookstore," they responded and asked if we couldn't have a bookstore for a dramatic play center. I am quite certain that very few of them have ever been in a bookstore, and there aren't many bookstores on TV. I'll never know the seed for this idea; but it was a rich learning opportunity for several weeks, not only in literacy but in math, counting and making change.

Ghosts and spirits, fishing, sewing, caring for babies, cooking, and building have all emerged as areas to include as home culture. The office, the bookstore, the hospital, the shampoo factory, the space toys have all emerged as pieces of the larger culture. Reading and writing (which for me in kindergarten include artistic representations) have become ways to explore, document, and preserve these activities.

When I think about what the very best kindergarten might be, I think it would have the natural rhythms of a home but more toys and kids. With this ideal, I have structured the environment and the day to enable the children to work and play for extended periods without adult intervention.

Closely observing the richness and depth of play has provided me with many more ideas of what can be included in the classroom for meaningful play. As I search for ways to help my children to develop literacy as a powerful tool to support their culture and as a means to become bicultural, I hope in some way to demonstrate that both traditional beliefs and the skills for living in, and critiquing, modern culture can co-exist in the same person.

Reference

Delpit, L. (1988). "The silenced dialogue: Power and pedagogy in educating other people's children." *Harvard Educational Review, 58*(3).

Kathleen Evans began her career as a teacher-director in a private early childhood school. She has directed public and private early childhood programs, taught kindergarten and first grade in urban schools, and is currently a literacy support teacher for Oakland Unified School District in Oakland, California. Kathleen is also involved in teacher training and staff development for the school district, as well as being adjunct faculty for Pacific Oaks College in Pasadena, California.

PLAY AND CULTURE

The Culture of Play:
A Personal Perspective

by Cheryl Greer Jarman

Some time ago, I was approached by a concerned teacher who wanted me to observe a child who, she said, was not engaging in dramatic play. The child, an African-American girl, was five; she was enrolled on a scholarship in a program attended primarily by dominant-culture, upper-middle-class children. The staff had been trying to find ways to connect the child with the environment and the other children.

When I observed, I saw most of the girls involved in house-keeping play — cooking, cleaning, taking care of the baby. Meanwhile, the child I was observing wandered around, picking up several different items for a few minutes, scanning books, and keeping an eye on the high level of activity. When she finally noticed me, she gave me *the look*. After a few moments, she came closer to me. I smiled and introduced myself. That was the icebreaker. She and I engaged in a lively conversation. I read a story to her, then another. We put a puzzle together. A few children asked me if I was her mother, and I proudly answered, "No, I am her friend."

When we talked later, the teacher was surprised at how open and involved this child had been with me. She had felt that the child was lacking in social skills. Taking a risk, I asked her, "Have you ever considered that housekeeping may not be play for her?" There was silence. I described some of the information the child had volunteered in our conversation; she described a home life that included many of what we call adult responsibili-ties. She had many tasks, which sometimes included child care roles. I suddenly realized that housekeeping wasn't play to her, it was work!

What a powerful thought, that every child does not view play through the eyes of her teacher! This scenario raised several issues for me regarding play: (1) What is play? (2) Who decides that it is play? (3) What is normative play?

And, lastly, (4) Whose values are honored as play is carried out?

It seems clear to me that what the teacher had interpreted as play was defined by the child as labor. It yielded no significant product. There was no optimism. That makes perfect sense to me! The real issue was that the teacher had an expectation, according to her value, that play should replicate something, that being in the housekeeping area was normative and being out of the mainstream activities was not. And because this child had a different concept, she was labeled as being deficient, unsociable, and needing *help*.

In an article I have written entitled "Caught Between Cultures, "I describe the disequilibrium that I experienced when I started school. Let me share with you a glimpse of my early school days.

"Space and boundaries were defined in a broader sense at home than at school. We, at meals, watched television, did homework, and entertained friends — all in the same room. Outside, it was not unusual to find a baseball game (using a broom handle and a tennis ball), hopscotch (drawn with a brick), bike riding, hand jives, and relay races concurrently happening in the space outside of my home called the street. We were all in it together, but it was your job to find a space for you and to watch out for cars.

At school, in contrast, I was reprimanded if I squeezed myself in on someone else's space. There were lines that told me where to go and where to play; everything was supposed to be done in a certain way. Games with already set-up rules were given to me as *play*. If we ran out of balls, I couldn't throw something else, even though there was plenty of sand. What are the rules of the school game?" (Greer, 1993, p. 61)

When I got to school, I knew how to play, but I *chose* not to play, until I found *my* play group. The activities that others were involved with, in a class in which there were only a few African-American children, didn't appeal to me. When I tried to involve myself in their play, I was often excluded or relegated to a menial role. I knew that I wasn't really wanted; I recognized the cues and body language that I was taught at an early age to be adept at identifying.

After a while, though, I found my group. Because they were Black like me, I assumed that we knew how to play together. In those days, almost every little Black child went to church. When you met someone, the first question was *What church do you go to?* Our play was initiated by that shared experience. In a Black Baptist church, kids saw a lot of things that tickled them — old ladies shouting "Thank you, Jesus!," preaching, weddings, funerals. But when we played church on the school playground, we got in trouble for all that shouting. There was always something wrong with us, something to be reprimanded for, something to stop doing, something for the teachers to be worried about.

Are we concerned when we see a group of children who are white playing together? Do we carefully watch their play? Do we assume that they don't know how to play if we don't see them with other children? Do we stop or question their choices of activities? Does their play give us comfort or make us feel uncomfortable?

James Banks has identified culture as having two main sections. Macroculture is our commonality; we share some national views and beliefs simply by all living in the same country. Beyond that, there is microculture, which is shared by specific group members. All of us belong to many other groups; and within the privacy and security of those groups, we are likely to view and interact with our world in a culturally appropriate manner. Thus, the task is to learn to function successfully and cooperatively within the macro and microcultures (Banks, 1989, p. 11) — to become bicultural.

What does this mean to children? I have described my confusion in my introduction to school. I had been very adept in playing in my own microculture. My play had been innovative, sociocentric, and fun. But when my microculture collided with the macroculture (and many school systems are structured around macroculture values), I did not fit. I was often punished for living, creating, and being myself.

In a working paper entitled "Children Learn Through Play," Betty Jones states:

"Observers in several parts of the world have described economically disadvantaged or minority-culture children as deficient in play skills. But there is evidence that children in unfamiliar settings both play and speak less freely. Spontaneous play and spontaneous language imply underlying knowledge of the "rules of the game," broadly defined. Children are competent in play when they are on familiar ground, using familiar words and materials and sharing a common set of expectations. Because all children are growing up in a multicultural world, play opportunities at school need to reproduce some of the diversity of that world and offer all children contact with both the familiar and the unfamiliar. If the school reflects only one culture and one language, then people not raised in that culture and language will be disadvantaged at school, and children who are raised in that culture and language will get no teachers' help in understanding the unfamiliar. It is important that teachers' help be given *in a play mode*, because that is how young children learn." (Jones, 1987)

Earlier, I cited some questions that I struggle with regarding play. They were my questions and now I would like to make them yours. How do you define play in your setting? Who decides that it is play in your setting? What is normative play in your setting? And whose values are honored in the play that is acceptable in your setting?

As educators, we have a responsibility to truly meet the needs of children, at *their* starting place. I am avidly against the deficit approach in teaching, which implies that children who are enacting their world in the context of their microculture in a macroculture setting need to be *fixed*. It is a model that I have often seen as I visit and observe in schools. Children who do not play within a DAP context, children who have ideas that are not valued, children who have not experienced and internalized the specific macroculture of school structure receive adult disapproval rather than support. It is a model that is sometimes used in parent/family work, primarily with parents and families who are considered minorities.

Our goal should not be *to fix*, our goal should be *to include*. Inclusion means provisioning and enriching the environment in a manner that fosters familiarity and unfamiliarity for each child. It means having an environment that helps children to *feel at home*, materials that they relate to, toys/games that have meaning for them. It supports play that they can invent, play that is valued because it was their choice. It is much easier to manipulate the environment than to manipulate the child.

Inclusion means abdication — giving up your vested power as a teacher and becoming a learner. I love watching children at play; I learn so much from them. Yet I feel a need to extend my knowledge beyond what they show me. If I want the environment to be familiar to them, then I have to know what they are familiar with. What is the cultural context of their play? How do they use the environment? How do they interact with each other? What do I know about their culture? Besides Erikson and Piaget, what theorists have I studied who have written about cultural and play patterns of non-European children? And lastly, have I viewed all children's play by the same standards? Whose play is assertive and whose is aggressive? Whose play is creative and whose is destructive? Whose play is individualistic and whose play is cooperative? Whose names always come up in staff meetings?

In summary, I challenge you to broaden your definition of developmentally appropriate practice. DAP means age appropriateness. DAP means individual appropriateness. But DAP includes cultural appropriateness — creating an environment that takes into account age, individual, and culture — the way a specific group views and interacts with the world. And that will truly be an environment that strives to meet the needs of all children.

References

Banks, J. A. (1989). Multicultural education: Characteristics and goals. In J. and C. Banks (editors), *Multicultural education: Issues and perspectives*. Boston: Allyn & Bacon.

Greer, C. (1993, November-December). "Caught between cultures." *Scholastic Early Childhood Today*, 60-61.

Jones, E. (1987). *Children learn through play: How do teachers support play?* Pasadena, CA: Pacific Oaks College: Unpublished working paper.

Cheryl Greer Jarman is a core faculty member at Pacific Oaks College in Pasadena, California. She is also a diversity consultant who specializes in early childhood and societal issues. Cheryl has written several articles and is a contributor to the acclaimed curriculum book, *Anti-Bias Curriculum: Tools for Empowering Young Children*. Cheryl is a regular presenter at conferences and she has a passion for the rights of children, spirituality, and the valuing of human rights.

PLAY AND CULTURE

"But They're Only Playing": Interpreting Play to Parents

by Renatta M. Cooper

Good practice in early childhood education, as defined by the progressive educators whose voices dominate the profession, emphasizes the role of play in a child's learning. This concept of play-based education is in conflict with the ideas that many parents have about the kind of education their children should have. Parent perspectives on play vary and are largely based on their own educational experiences, social class, and cultural norms and values.

African-American parents typically have very fundamentalist values when it comes to the education of their children. Both parents who were successful and those who were unsuccessful in school themselves are skeptical of educational innovations that appear trendy or lacking in substance. School is for work; and if you work hard, it can help you get ahead.

Immigrants from Mexico, Central America, and South America often share a view of "the *educación* of their children, that is, raising them to be responsible members of society as they understand it" (Valdés, 1996, p. 180).

School, in this value system, is not for playing around. It is where you practice obedience, respect, and the work ethic. In both African-American and Latino cultural models, play is considered an amusing part of childhood; but it isn't viewed as part of the learning process.

In an increasingly hostile nation, parents from oppressed groups are suspicious of anything that may reduce their child's competitiveness in the job market. In families that view play as *messing around*, there is scant acceptance of play as a legitimate part of curriculum (Cooper, 1996, p. 94).

For good reasons, parents from one cultural background may be uninclined to trust a teacher from a different background to have their child's interests at heart. "How can she really know what's best for my child?" It takes a leap of faith to trust a teacher who tells you that play is important but can't demonstrate why this is so, or how play will benefit your child in the future. If you want parents to trust you as an educator, you'd better be able to demonstrate the importance of play in a convincing manner. This requires strong curriculum building and planning, designing play environments that support learning and then explaining to parents how they work (Cooper, 1996, p. 94).

Strong observational skills are crucial. As a teacher, I often stood next to a parent as we observed her child, discussing what we were seeing in terms of problem solving, motor skills, or language development. Parents were often enthralled; I was a trained observer, they were not, and initially they didn't see what I saw. However, as I shared my observations with them, they began to develop a new appreciation for play skills and to see play with new eyes. As a result, they not only began to trust me as an educator, as someone knowledgeable about and committed to their child's growth, but they also began to understand their child's learning process. Parents' own memories tend to recall school as important but boring. If they can discover learning as fun as well as substantive, they will be willing to accept a play-based curriculum.

They will accept it with more confidence if some of the trappings of school are present, even in classrooms for four and five year olds. A writing center which offers spontaneous practice with school tools — paper, pens and pencils, crayons and markers, scissors and staplers — can include letter and number stencils, *key word* cards, blank books to create stories in, note pads, and clipboards, and an attentive adult ready to listen to children's stories and write them down. Manipulatives with built-in shapes and colors, puzzles, even simple worksheets that can be used to *play school* without having to meet too-demanding expectations for accuracy — these things look like school. Books, too, are familiar parts of school, and children to whom adults read often will also *read* to each other playfully, practicing page turning, left-to-right sequencing, and story memory as they do so.

More vigorous play may require interpretation to parents in terms of skill learning. When children are exploring sand, water, woodworking, blocks, what skills and concepts are they developing? A teacher can report her observations to parents, adding details about language development and social problem solving and cooperation. Pay attention to what parents value and look for examples of those behaviors by their child, in order to assure them that this school supports their values and values their child.

This isn't always easy. As one example, adult-child ratios may make it easy to ignore individual children, especially those a teacher finds unrewarding for reasons of language, appearance, cultural or personal style. It is difficult for most teachers to admit that they are *put off* by certain children entrusted to their care. Teachers are human, however, and they are products of a society that targets certain groups with abundant negative stereotypes. It is healthier, and more accurate, to be open to the idea that you have been affected by such negative stereotypes and biases. Once confronted, biases can be changed. Bias that is denied continues to develop.

The jockeying for position and friendship that goes on in any peer group may work against a child from a non-dominant cultural group who doesn't know the rules of their *game*. Some children simply withdraw; others do whatever is necessary to get attention from other children and from adults. As children try to establish themselves in a peer group, showing off is frequently an effective strategy to get other children to pay attention to oneself. Teachers may disapprove — but even negative adult attention can be more satisfying than no attention. Some children are more noticed by teachers when they misbehave than they are when they are doing what they should do.

A strategy I used in the classroom, that was a concrete useful way to monitor the type of interactions I had with the children I worked with, was to have a set of index cards with a child's name on each card. At the end of the program day, by myself or with my co-teachers, we would go through the cards and determine whether this child was interacted with today. What kind of interaction was it? Instructive? Corrective? Collaborative? This system helped us ensure that each child got quality, pleasant interactions from everyone. This can be done quickly, or with a long discussion focusing on each child in depth when you have more time.

Differences in cultural and physical styles often create misunderstandings. Everyone's memories of school include an emphasis on being still and quiet. Few young children are capable of still and quiet, nor do they learn much without being physically and verbally engaged. And four year old boys may represent the height of human activity levels! Hale, in her book *Black Children* (1986), has reminded us of the high kinesthetic skill levels typical of African-American young children:

"Harry Morgan (1976) points out that Black children are motorically precocious. They are more active and have more physical energy to expend than white children. Morgan maintains that the schools do not support the natural energy level of Black children. He suggests that Black children need an active environment for successful learning, particularly lower-income children whose grandparents emphasize survival skills rather than conformity, docility, and quiet manners — more typical of middle-class child-rearing" (Hale, 1986, p. 75).

Middle-class African-American mothers may downplay their children's motoric precocity and not seek to extend it because development in this area might interfere with their children's school behavior and performance.

But active Black children, especially male children, often have female teachers who are not Black and who have been subtly socialized to be alert to possible aggression from Black males. The likelihood is very high that teachers will be especially aware of, and unconsciously expecting trouble from, the few Black children in a primarily white or otherwise mixed group.

The likelihood that these children, when in need of guidance, will receive mixed messages is also very high. White middle-class women aren't supposed to act angry even when they are. They're supposed to stay sweetly reasonable with children. Children accustomed to clearer messages and firmer rules may not understand *soft* discipline and keep pushing to discover where the limits really are in this strange place. ("If you're my teacher, can you keep me safe?") Cynthia Ballenger is an experienced European-American preschool teacher who found herself incapable of effective group management ("The children ran me ragged.") when she began working with Black children from Haiti, whose culture was unfamiliar to her. To become effective, she had to learn to listen to the Haitian adults in their effective interactions with the children. (1992)

We all have much to learn from each other. Effective teaching, when cultural differences make us stumble, requires very close attention to understand what's going on with a child. Most teachers aren't open to looking at their own hidden expectations. There is more safety in avoiding children (and parents) whose language we don't speak, whose cues we don't catch. When the children catch us at avoidance and make us pay

The following strategies may help in supporting both children and parents:

- Observe children as they play, to *catch them being good* — to identify their individual strengths and interests. Give them attention that acknowledges these assets.

- Interpret children's accomplishments to their parents. Find out parents' goals for their children and emphasize children's growth toward those goals in your conversations with parents.

- Keep learning about the development of language and literacy in early childhood — since literacy is at the heart of the elementary school curriculum, the next challenge your children will encounter. Provide many activities for open-ended exploration of language and all the forms of literacy — drawing, building, dramatizing, as well as writing and reading.

- Share with parents, and children, your own belief in the value of education and in their ability to succeed in school. Some working-class parents may not know anyone who has been helped by going to school; you do. What success stories can you tell?

- Be upfront about the rules of the "culture power" (Delpit, 1988). I admire a colleague, Molly Scudder, who featured *playing first grade* in the second half of her kindergarten year. Following rules didn't replace the critical thinking and problem-solving characteristics of her class; rather, it became a new topic for lively discussion, as she asked children to practice lining up, complete with boys' and girls' lines, and being "so quiet that nobody hears us coming."

"Why?" asked these children, and the question was taken seriously and brainstormed. Learning conforming behaviors because they please people in power, because those things are important to some people, gives children an important set of survival strategies to be consciously exercised if they choose to do so.

attention, we are likely to overreact and blame the child — or his parents.

The discrimination inherent in our society enables us to stay unaware of these patterns, unless we work at becoming aware of our own biases. The basic focus in early childhood education — identify and build on each child's strengths — can serve us well here. By observing children at play, we get to know them.

References

Ballenger, C. (1992). "Because you like us: The language of control." *Harvard Educational Review, 62*(2), 199-208.

Cooper, R. M. (1996). "The role of play in the acculturation process." In A. L. Philips (editor), *Playing for keeps* (pp. 89-98). St. Paul, MN: Redleaf Press.

Delpit, L. (1988). "The silenced dialogue: Power and pedagogy in educating other people's children." *Harvard Educational Review, 58*(3).

Hale, J. (1986). *Black children: Their roots, culture and learning style.* New York: Teachers College Press.

Valdés, G. (1996). *Con respeto.* Baltimore, MD: The Johns Hopkins University Press.

Renatta M. Cooper is the Education Coordinator/Program Specialist for the Los Angeles County Office of Child Care. Her areas of expertise include negotiating educational systems for non-traditional students, early childhood education, bicultural development, and play. She is the co-author of the Teacher's College Press publication *Playing to Get Smart*. Renatta is a former Commissioner of First 5 LA, a former faculty member at Pacific Oaks College, and was the founding director of the Jones Prescott Institute/Hixon Center for Early Childhood Education at Pacific Oaks.

Understanding Culture Through Play

by Gretchen Reynolds

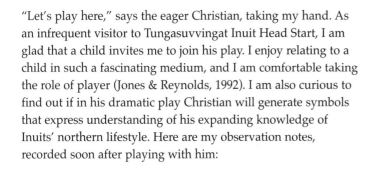

"Let's play here," says the eager Christian, taking my hand. As an infrequent visitor to Tungasuvvingat Inuit Head Start, I am glad that a child invites me to join his play. I enjoy relating to a child in such a fascinating medium, and I am comfortable taking the role of player (Jones & Reynolds, 1992). I am also curious to find out if in his dramatic play Christian will generate symbols that express understanding of his expanding knowledge of Inuits' northern lifestyle. Here are my observation notes, recorded soon after playing with him:

I quickly discover that my companion is a capable pretend player. In the short time we play together, Christian switches roles easily — he is a daddy, mommy, baby, and fish, and he encourages me to play multiple roles as well. Christian's play reveals knowledge of traditional Inuit lifestyle and, with the encouragement of his teacher, he uses some Inuktitut vocabulary.

The Tungasuvvingat Inuit Head Start

. . . urban areas present special challenges for the survival of aboriginal cultures. These challenges come in part because many of the traditional sources of aboriginal culture — contact with the land, elders, aboriginal languages, and spiritual ceremonies — are difficult to maintain in cities at present. Moreover, aboriginal people are continuously exposed to perceptions, either consciously or unconsciously held, that cities are not where aboriginal cultures belong and can flourish. (Peters, 1996, p. 321)

The Tungasuvvingat Inuit Head Start Program has been open for almost two years. Funded by Health Canada under the Aboriginal Head Start Initiative, its mission is described this way. "The retention of the Inuit culture and Inuktitut language is paramount in this program. Curriculum activities and materials, special events, daily snacks, parent education and parent resources should reflect the Inuit culture whenever possible. Inuktitut will be considered an official language of the program and will be promoted throughout all activities during the day. It is also the policy of the program to employ Inuit staff as much as possible." (*Parent Handbook*, 1997, p. 2)

The Inuit were formerly called Eskimo people. They traditionally live in the Arctic regions, although now there are many Inuit dwelling in urban communities in Canada. There are approximately 500 Inuit living in Ottawa, a populous, industrialized city thousands of miles away from the environment that is indigenous to their culture. The children's parents speak one or both of Canada's two official languages, English and French; but many do not use their primary language, Inuktitut, because families and individuals have gradually relocated to cities for employment, and the experience of residential schooling has contributed to the loss of ethnic languages. They want to retain their culture and their primary language, and so they believe this program is an important beginning for their children. Liz Lightford, the program coordinator, tells me, "I think being in the south is a heartache for some parents. For Inuit, family is important to them, and home is important. So when they're away from home, even though they choose to be in Ottawa, the homesickness that they feel is a real heartache. So they want their kids to have some of home in the city, and it's a way of passing on themselves through their kids even though the children can't be in the north learning it traditionally." (Lightford, 1997).

Children learn culture by playing it

Vygotsky's sociocultural theory of learning suggests that children construct knowledge within a cultural context through social interactions with adults and peers. The result is particular skills and learning that is valued by a culture. The theory also emphasizes the concept that symbols — all the various ways that meaning is represented by human beings, including spoken language — are the tools for conveying meaning and influencing the surrounding environment (Berk & Winsler, 1995). Dramatic play is a symbol system that young children use naturally and comfortably.

According to Vygotsky, imaginary play is the child's growing edge — in play, the child is stretched to behave a head taller than him or herself. Imaginative play is the most effective context for stimulating a young child's cognitive development because he or she uses symbols to communicate meaning to other players (Berk & Winsler, 1995). In play, the child recreates experience by using symbols that reflect the cultural milieu. Play is socially constructed and dynamic, as children negotiate meanings "seamlessly" from within the frame of the play.

Can children learn culture through play? What is the role of the teacher? These questions are the motive for my visits to the Tungasuvvingat Inuit Head Start, where I discover how teachers in a setting for urban Inuit children are using a rich environment, thoughtful teaching interventions, and quality play to cultivate children's knowledge of their Inuit roots.

The play environment

Liz is a European Canadian from Ottawa. In speaking to her about the issues for teachers wanting to implement cultural curriculum, Liz articulates their concern. "One of our challenges is to replicate culture authentically in every part of the curriculum. How can we ensure that all the components of the program, including curriculum, room arrangement, behavior guidance, and transitions, are not a token acknowledgment of culture, but are real, authentic, and meaningful?" (Lightford, 1997)

The environment at Tungasuvvingat Inuit Head Start contains some familiar early childhood education equipment. There are blocks, Legos®, puzzles, supplies for writing and drawing, and a wheelchair for dolls. The new computer is ever popular, for one child or several children working side by side.

My eye is attracted to the array of materials and objects suggestive of northern themes and/or used by Inuit people. The book corner contains a shelf filled with children's books in Inuktitut (a few have English translations) and stuffed animals commonly found in the Arctic. Dulled ulus (women's knives) are available at the play dough table. In the block corner, a child helps herself to several miniature rubber seals, a dolphin, and a whale, which she carefully arranges on a child-sized kamutiik (Arctic sled) and pulls across the middle of the room. Looking towards the dramatic play area, I see dolls with brown skin, dark hair, and dark eyes; a child-sized amauti (a traditional baby-carrying parka); kamiik (Inuit boots); and caribou skins. In the music corner, the children play Inuit drums or they can listen to aiyaya songs and throat singing on tape. Inuktitut syllabics decorate the walls and a set of colorful homemade alphabet blocks. The children's names are in Inuktitut and English in their cubbies. A water table contains sea green water, a large rock and pebbles, a sea turtle and dolphins, and several big clam shells.

Child-teacher interactions

Ina Kuluguqtuq is the children's Inuk teacher, and her first language is Inuktitut. Eight or nine children gather with Ina on the rug. She has a small blue and white crocheted bag in her lap. "This was my favorite game when I was a little girl." Ina ties a long piece of nylon rope to form a loop at one end and pokes the open loop into the bag. She pulls the drawstring, closing the bag tight. Engaging a ritual, she shakes the bag, chanting, "Sha la la la la la!" The children watch, fascinated. Then Ina hitches the nylon rope tight, pulling out a handful of small bones caught in the loop.

"Let's see what kind of friends I got!" Separating them and naming them one by one, according to size, Ina exclaims, "I have anaana (mom). I have panik (girl). I have another girl. And this is ataata (dad). Three girls, a baby girl, and an ataata." All the children are eager to have a turn, and they wait patiently as Ina gives every child a chance to play the bone game. Whenever someone shakes the crocheted bag, children merrily join the incantation, "Sha la la la la la!" The energy for the bone game wanes, but it is left out for children to play with during the morning.

A Head Start in Inuit identity

My documentation of the play at the Tungasuvvingat Inuit Head Start is a small window on many things Inuit children are learning about their indigenous culture. Children's curiosity is stimulated in an environment containing an array of strange and wonderful objects from the culture and toys suggestive of Inuit lifestyle. Children have access to people with a history of living with the objects and who want to explain and demonstrate their use.

Ina takes out a big piece of dried caribou sinew. "What's that, Ina?" the ever curious, four year old Christian wants to know.

It's a thread for making clothing," is Ina's reply. Christian watches as Ina breaks off a long, thread-like piece. She continues, "You know what, my dad used this to clean his teeth. He goes like this." Holding the thread close to her mouth, Ina makes exaggerated flossing motions. They giggle.

Christian imitates his teacher's flossing gesture and then asks for a try with the real thing. Christian experiments for several minutes to make the hairy, distasteful piece of caribou sinew work in the spaces between his teeth.

Ina describes how the opportunity to work with children to learn about Inuit traditions is bringing back many memories:

. . . today, when I am trying to plan, trying to think about our Inuit ways, my grandma is coming back. They (memories) are coming back to me since we started this program, gradually they're coming back.

Ina explains the tremendous pleasure for her in using her native language every day:

To me, the language is everything. If I don't speak my language for about a week. let's say I speak only English, I'm craving for something, and I know exactly what I'm craving for, speaking in my mother tongue. When I speak Inuktitut, I just relax again, my muscles were all uptight. It's very important, my language. It's always in me, I always speak it, especially around here, and when I see other Inuit I feel more special, especially living down south. When I'm in an English setting, I feel smaller. I feel like I have two sides, one side in English, and one in Inuktitut. That's why so many of us Inuit are losing our language. When we've been down here for long, we're just stuck in English, because we don't hear Inuktitut anymore. When I'm speaking my mother tongue, I feel strong. (Kuluguqtuq, 1997).

Elaine, the children's other aboriginal teacher, says, "I don't speak Inuktitut, but I'm feeling very soothed that it's around me because it's a sadness in my heart that I don't speak. Especially in the Ottawa area, no one speaks enough of their own language, so there's sadness over that. So when I hear it here, I know it's one big strong community. And now the children are feeling very comfortable with it." (Shipley, 1997)

The children have an exceptional opportunity here to develop a sense of themselves as special, different, and uniquely Inuit. Derman-Sparks (et al., 1989) suggests that the first task in classrooms with children of color is to build their sense of personal and group identity. Phillips emphasizes that the transformation to self-identity cannot be assumed by outsiders. People ". . . of color work toward reclaiming and affirming their racial group identity, and therefore themselves, where the new identity is based on their group's definition of themselves, not the dominant group's definition" (Phillips, 1998, p. 58). Immersion in their culture for several years is assurance that these children will have a head start in the development of a strong Inuit identity. A play-based curriculum supports that goal because good play empowers young children.

At play, both children and adults are challenged to invent new solutions to problems within flexible rules and rapidly changing scripts. Playing together, they practice negotiating their varied *worldviews to create mutually satisfactory and increasingly complex understandings of their lives. In so doing, children are mastering skills and dispositions that they will need throughout their lives.* (Jones & Reynolds, 1995, p. 45)

Resources

Berk, L., & Winsler, A. (1995). *Scaffolding children's learning: Vygotsky and early childhood education*. Washington, DC: National Association for the Education of Young Children.

Derman-Sparks, L., & ABC Task Force (1989). *Anti-bias curriculum*. Washington, DC: National Association for the Education of Young Children.

Jones, E., & Reynolds, G. (1992). *The play's the thing: Teachers' roles in children's play*. New York: Teachers College Press.

Jones, E., & Reynolds, G. (1995). "Enabling children's play: The teacher's role." In E. Klugman (editor), *Play, policy, and practice* (pp. 37-46). St. Paul, MN: Redleaf Press.

Kuluguqtuq, I. (1997). Personal communication.

Lightford, L. (1997). Personal communication.

Peters, E. (1996). "Aboriginal people in urban areas." In D. A. Long and O. P. Dickason (editors), *Visions of the heart: Canadian aboriginal issues* (pp. 305-333). Toronto: Harcourt Brace & Company, Canada.

Phillips, C. B. (1998). "Preparing teachers to use their voices for change." *Young Children*, 53(3), 55-60.

Shipley, E. (1997). Personal communication.

Tungasuvvingat Inuit Head Start (1997, March). *Parent handbook*. Ottawa: Author.

The material in this article appears in a casebook on play to accompany *Playing for Keeps*, a 1996 publication of Redleaf Press.

Some of this material appeared in "Welcoming Place: An Urban Community of Inuit Families," in *Canadian Children: Journal of the Canadian Association for Young Children*, Spring/Printemps 1998, Volume 23, Number 1.

Gretchen Reynolds is on the faculty in the early childhood education program at Algonquin College in Ottawa, Ontario, and adjunct faculty teaching online courses at Pacific Oaks College in Pasadena, California.